Social Security Policy in Britain

Social Security Policy in Britain

Michael Hill

Professor of Social Policy
The University of Newcastle upon Tyne

Edward Elgar

Published by
Edward Elgar Publishing Limited
Gower House
Croft Road
Aldershot
Hants GU11 3HR
England

Edward Elgar Publishing Company
Old Post Road
Brookfield
Vermont 05036
USA

British Library Cataloguing in Publication Data

Hill, Michael, *1937-*
    Social security policy in Britain.
    1. Great Britain. Social security benefits. Policies of government,
        history
    I. Title
    386.400941

ISBN 1 85278 300 1
        1 85278 305 2 (paperback)

Typeset in Great Britain by Inhit Limited, Godalming, Surrey
and printed by Billing & Sons Ltd, Worcester

Contents

v

Figures and Tables

FIGURES

TABLES

Preface

My understanding of social security policy, and therefore perhaps
my approach to analysing it, was developed during four years as
an Executive Officer in a local office of the National Assistance
Board. Academic analysis of it came later. In those formative
years I owed a great deal to Tony Lynes who helped me to think
about my practical experience. Next, I owe a special debt to Olive
Stevenson who enabled me to become involved in research on
social security policy. Two other people whom I would like to
thank for helping me to develop my thinking over many years are
Adrian Sinfield and Peter Townsend. Additionally, in the 1970s,
David Donnison provided me with some excellent opportunities
to become involved in discussions on social security policy; and I
currently am especially indebted to Geoff Fimister, who works
with me on short courses and gives me the benefit of his considerable experience as a welfare rights officer and as an adviser to the
local government associations. These are, however, but a few of
the many people upon whose experience I have been able to draw
over the years: civil servants, welfare rights officers, local government housing benefit staff and, of course, fellow academics and
researchers. I hope these others will accept my general thanks;
they are far too many to name.

I would also like to thank both my wife Betty and Sue Ward for
their careful scrutiny of the manuscript. The latter's deep knowledge of pensions was particularly helpful; although I fear that the
manuscript still does not deal fully enough with the complexities
of public–private interactions in the pensions field, it would have
been weaker still without Sue's help.

Alan and Rosemary Towers have done an excellent job in
preparing the manuscript, despite having to work initially with
indistinct and rambling tapes which they miraculously transformed
into punctuated typescript. Finally, I would like to thank Edward
Elgar for encouraging me to write the book and, of course, for
publishing it.

1. Introduction

This book examines the current state of British social security policy, and explains options for the future, and will look at current policies in context, examining their history and exploring the political factors which have influenced their character. It uses a policy analysis approach which emphasizes the need to understand the political processes which have shaped our policies, and the need to situate any proposals for reform of these policies within a realistic assessment of the political, social, economic context. This approach to the study of policy concerns itself not merely with the forces which shape policy but also with ways in which policy is implemented. In the course of doing this it gives attention to the many significant interactions between social security policy and other public policies.

Clearly, a book about British social security policy needs to start with some explanation of the way in which the concept of social security is used. In Britain it has become customary to use the expression 'social security' to embrace the whole range of state income maintenance policies. Overall, the definition of social security may be identified with the range of policy responsibilities of the government's Department of Social Security which operates through a system of local offices, to which individuals may apply for both insurance and for means-tested benefits. The Department also assumes responsibility for the system of housing benefits, providing support for the rents and local tax payments of low-income people. Housing benefit is paid by local government but policy is made by, and the system is supervised by, the central Department of Social Security.

Furthermore, the Department also takes responsibility for social security schemes operated by employers and by private organizations: statutory sick and maternity pay, and pensions schemes regulated under the laws which allow individuals to opt to contract out of part of the state system.

However, whilst those policies which are the responsibility of the Department of Social Security will be the central concerns of this book, it is important to recognize that these central social security policies interact in significant ways with other public policies. One cannot consider the contribution of the state to income maintenance without giving consideration to other policies which may affect individual income and well-being. In particular, there is a wide range of ways in which social security interacts with taxation policies. Policies which provide relief from taxation under certain circumstances – for example, relief from taxation of mortgage interest payments or pension contributions – have an important impact upon individual incomes and therefore cannot be considered entirely separately from the more direct income maintenance policies.

In the field of housing, overall, it is important to bear in mind that public policies alternatively provide direct help to low-income rent-payers, subsidies for housebuyers, controls over the levels of rent which people may be charged and subsidies to the cost of providing housing. Each of these policies makes contributions towards, or has an effect on, individual housing costs and therefore may have implications for the more direct subsidies of income offered by way of social security.

It is similarly important to recognize that, wherever the state provides subsidies to services or benefits in kind, this again makes a contribution of some sort towards income maintenance. The examples in this category are legion: in education, health services, transport, the arts, recreation, even sport, and so on. It is not suggested that our examination of social security has to delve deeply into these policies but merely that interactions with them must not be overlooked. It must be realized that access to free or subsidized services makes a contribution to individual incomes. It is important to bear in mind that political choices have been made about whether to provide these services on a universal and comparatively cheap basis, or to provide them to some individuals at full cost while subsidizing them for low-income groups on a means-tested basis, or to provide them at full cost and compensate low-income people through social security policies to enable them to be able to purchase them. Poverty implies not simply a lack of resources, but difficulties in securing access to benefits and services which higher-income people enjoy (see Townsend 1979; Mack and Lansley 1985). Political efforts to alleviate it, or to modify income inequalities in general, may involve both the direct enhancement of lower incomes and the indirect provision of benefits and services in kind. Such political choices may imply a need for discussion about the most appropriate strategies, taking into account both egalitarian objectives and devices to ensure that specific services are accessible and available to all (see discussion in Le Grand 1982).

When studying social security policy it is also important to remember that, alongside state provision, we find forms of, first, individual provision by way of private pension and insurance arrangements; second, provision explicitly related to, and perhaps subsidized by employers; and, third, forms of collective action through trades unions, friendly societies and other community arrangements to enable individuals to cope with income maintenance problems. These provisions are not necessarily entirely independent of the state. The state may subsidize some of these modes of individual provision, either directly through contributions to specific schemes or indirectly through tax reliefs. Even if it does not subsidize them, the state may play a role in underwriting such schemes, in securing a legal framework within which individuals' rights may be guaranteed under these schemes, and in preventing fraudulent operation of schemes. In most countries a mixture of public and private social security will be found, with some important policy issues likely to be present about the relationship between the two systems. In the British case the most important example of this phenomenon is the coexistence of public and private pension schemes. As with state benefits, it is important to recognize that private schemes may provide both benefits in cash and benefits in kind or in services.

Finally, it is important to bear in mind that any structure of social security policies needs to be seen in a broader economic context. Social security measures are generally perceived as required because market-related economic processes generate inequalities, with consequences in terms of individual deprivation which are deemed to be politically unacceptable, either because of the threat they pose for social order or because of political movements and ideologies which demand remedial measures. But, an attack on these inequalities may take forms which do not involve social security measures, or at least do not depend upon social security alone. Low wages and unemployment, for example, may be compensated by social security benefits but they may equally be attacked by incomes policies, guaranteed wages policies and measures to enhance employment. Again, there is a range of ways in which policies of this kind interact with social security policies which must be given consideration.

To sum up these introductory observations, this book has been described as being concerned with state social security policies in Britain. But, in considering these policies, it cannot disregard other policies, both public and private, which influence individual incomes and wellbeing. It will therefore have to give some attention to interactions between social security and these other policies. Furthermore, when in the later chapters it moves on to issues for the future, it will raise questions about the extent to which advances in policies to protect individuals from poverty, or to reduce inequalities, will or should come in the form of social security policies or in the form of other kinds of public policy interventions in society.

Having identified, in general terms, the subject matter of this book, the rest of this chapter will discuss various approaches to the study of social security. It is divided into four sections. The first of these deals with what is described as the 'social administration' approach. The second looks at the economics-based approach to the subject. The third looks at the way in which political science contributes to the study of social security policy. The last section discusses what is described as the 'implementation approach' concerned to examine how the system works.

THE SOCIAL ADMINISTRATION APPROACH

This approach to the study of social security is called the social administration approach in recognition of the very important contribution to the study of social policy made by academic researchers, many of whom have been located in university departments of social administration or social policy. Dominating this approach was Richard Titmuss who led a team of teachers and researchers at the London School of Economics in the 1940s, 1950s and 1960s (see Titmuss 1958: 1968). However, the approach to the study of social security which will be described in this section has its origins in studies of poverty, and of policies for the relief of poverty initiated in the last years of the nineteenth century. Characteristically this approach sees poverty and inequality as a problem for society. It lays its emphasis on presenting the facts about poverty and about its relief to persuade society to take action. Implicit in this approach is a belief in the importance of accurately measuring and recording the evidence on poverty to demonstrate the need for a social, and implicitly a governmental, response to the problem. It is an approach that lays a strong emphasis upon rationality, and upon the need to demonstrate the facts. It also manifests a strong dependence upon the moral strength of its case, upon a belief that once the facts are known people will recognize the importance of taking action. This approach has strong roots in liberal democratic social philosophies, with their concerns about social solidarity and about the extent of collective responsibility for the needs of individuals.

The nineteenth-century roots of this approach lay in the studies of poverty carried out by Charles Booth (1903) in London and Seebohm Rowntree in York (Rowntree 1901, 1941; Rowntree and Lavers 1951). These studies made an important contribution towards the recognition of the continuing existence of poverty in Britain, at a time when industrialization had created a generally prosperous nation in which many people's living standards were rising very rapidly. The authors of these studies, the researchers who worked with them, and the politicians and philanthropists influenced by their work drew upon them to argue for the development of specific state policies to meet the problems of poverty. They developed arguments for new kinds of social security policies which went beyond the very limited response to need already provided by the Poor Law.

These early studies initiated a tradition of social investigation in Britain, which was essentially pragmatic and problem-oriented. The Fabian Society played an important role in the first half of the twentieth century in arguing for the systematic study of social issues. Researchers like Bowley (Bowley and Burnett-Hurst 1915; Bowley and Hogg 1925) developed more sophisticated studies built upon the work of the pioneers. Departments in some of the universities, notably the London School of Economics and the Universities of Birmingham and Liverpool, were established to carry forward the study of social policy issues. The persistent unemployment of the interwar period gave further impetus to studies of this kind.

In the postwar period, as has already been mentioned, Richard Titmuss was very active in developing the study of poverty and social security at the London School of Economics. In the 1950s, Titmuss and his colleagues began to challenge the complacency which seemed to be developing in Britain about the welfare state measures introduced in the 1940s. To Richard Titmuss and his colleagues, Brian Abel-Smith and Peter Townsend, have been attributed what is sometimes described as 'the rediscovery of poverty' in studies carried out at the end of the 1950s and in the early 1960s which demonstrated the many loopholes in the social security provisions enacted by the Labour government in the 1940s (Abel-Smith and Townsend 1965). This academic work led to efforts to persuade the Labour Party that, when it next came to power, it would need to enact measures to build upon its past social security measures. It also led to the development of pressure-group activities to try to secure an adequate governmental response to problems of poverty. The pressure group which has most effectively carried forward the social administration approach into British political life is the Child Poverty Action Group, set up in 1965. This group has become an important source of data on the inadequacies of social security policy (McCarthy 1986).

I, myself, have been considerably influenced by the social administration approach, and would not wish to disassociate myself from its powerful commitment to rationality and to the moral case against inequality. However, it must be recognized that those influenced by this tradition have, at times, tended to underestimate the political forces ranged against them. The belief that the facts speak for themselves may involve a failure to identify the essential political weakness of the poor, and the difficulties of getting issues about the relief of poverty on to the political agenda. Whatever the moral strength of the case, there are enormous difficulties about arguing for greater government expenditure upon social security when social security expenditure already dominates public expenditure. Policy advocates in this tradition have consistently argued for the further development of the universalist model of social security provision, building upon the work of Beveridge, whilst, at least since the 1970s, changes to the causes of poverty and to government social security policies have systematically undermined that model. Control over the political agenda is likely to lie in the hands of individuals with other concerns and preoccupations. Other advisers, whose arguments for social security policies are more sharply related to concerns about the 'efficient' expenditure of public money, and about the relationship between social security expenditure and other government activities to strengthen and sustain the economy are likely to be more dominant. We turn to the contribution of this group in the next section.

THE ECONOMICS APPROACH

Whilst the social administration tradition has had a very central concern with public social security policy in Britain, we cannot find amongst the economics profession more than a rather minor subsidiary concern with the working of social security policy. However, the economics approach has been identified separately in this book because it has certain characteristics which are important for policy analysis. It shares with the social administration approach a concern with policy rationality, but its approach to policy rationality can be said to be dominated by a concern with the twin concepts of *efficiency* and *effectiveness*, which are then applied to the analysis of policy. Efficiency is concerned with the relationship between outputs and inputs – a concern about maximizing gains whilst minimizing costs. Effectiveness goes further than this in concerning itself with the extent to which policies increase welfare. But what is also important about the economics approach is the extent to which it concerns itself with the contribution of a policy not merely to the alleviation of individual problems but to the advancement of the general good. This leads it to ask questions about the extent to which there is an efficient relationship between the resources taken away from some individuals in order to benefit other individuals. The concern here, then, is with issues about net gains to society, and hard questions may therefore be raised about the extent to which public redistributive policies have consequences which are disadvantageous for the economy as a whole, and accordingly (it is argued) disadvantageous for the general good.

Not very surprisingly most economic analysis in a capitalist society rests upon assumptions about the overall superiority of the capitalist model for the organization of economic activity, seeing public intervention as justifiable inasmuch as there are believed to be correctable imperfections in the model (tendencies towards monopoly, collective action problems to be solved, external effects of entrepreneurial activity and so on). Where the social administration approach therefore tends to take for granted public interventions towards the relief of poverty and the alleviation of inequalities, the economics approach is likely to involve the asking of questions about the consequences of such interventions for the working of the free market. Of course, economic analysts differ in their complacency about capitalism, but it is taken to be the overall hallmark of this approach that it sees the relationship between social security interventions and the working of the economy as of key importance. The economics approach will tend to be identified, in this book, with methods of providing social security benefits which minimize costs and concentrate benefits on carefully identified groups of needy people: selective rather than universalist policies. However, this should not be taken to imply that all professional economists are advocates of selectivity. On the contrary there are examples of economists who have made an important contribution to the case for universalism and the exposure of problems about selectivity (see, for example, Atkinson 1969).

The economics approach to the study of social security policy tends to focus upon issues about the place of social security policy within public expenditure policy in general, and about issues about the impact of measures for the relief of poverty upon economic behaviour and particularly labour market behaviour (see, for example, McClements 1978; Dilnot, Kay and Morris 1984). However, notwithstanding the reservation about the above generalization, it is fair to say that an important feature of the economics approach has been its strong emphasis upon the targeting of social security policies. Advocates from this school of thought have therefore become very involved in examining ways of integrating taxation and benefits and ways of developing means tests. By contrast to those influenced by the social administration approach, who have argued that general entitlements to benefit contribute to social solidarity, minimize stigma and maximize take-up of help by poor people, this group of students of the social security system have tended to emphasize what they see as the inefficiency of universal benefit systems.

The flaw in the approach to rationality used by this group of students of the social security system lies in a belief that policies operate exactly in the way in which they are intended to operate, and in the belief that citizens all behave as 'rational economic individuals' fully informed about the options available to them and able and willing to make calculations about the forms of behaviour that will benefit them most efficiently. Economists also tend at times to share with those who come to the subject from the social administration perspective a naivety about the political processes which actually determine policy. Their naivety consists in a belief that considerations of efficiency and effectiveness will dominate the political decision-making process.

THE POLITICAL SCIENCE APPROACH

Both the social administration approach and the economics approach to our subject involve a concern with policy advocacy; by contrast the political science approach to the subject is concerned to explain the system we have got, and to look at the political forces which have determined its shape and structure. Of course students of social security policy in this tradition may have strong views about the strengths and weaknesses of present policy, and strong views about the policies that should be adopted, but the contribution of their discipline to the subject is limited to an explanatory role. However, explanation is important in order to reach a realistic assessment of both those forces which support the present system and those which may be ranged against attempts to change it in new directions.

The political science approach to this subject may be subdivided into various more specific approaches according to theoretical perspective. There is, above all, a distinct divide between the neo-Marxist approach to the explanation of the social security system, which looks at it in terms of its functions for the capitalist economy and state, and the liberal pluralist approach, which is concerned with the roles of electoral forces, pressure groups and professional interests in explaining policy content. The first of these approaches may indeed be described separately as the 'political economy' approach to the study of social security, to distinguish it from the more limited kind of explanation of the political system provided by the liberal–pluralist approach.

The neo-Marxist, or political economy, approach raises questions about the role social security plays in both enabling a capitalist economic system to work more efficiently, and in reducing the propensity of individuals to engage in activities which would threaten the capitalist economy (see Gough 1979; or Novak 1984, 1988, for example). It has its roots in the requirement of theorists in the Marxist tradition to explain why Karl Marx's predictions about the increased polarization between capitalists and proletariat have not come about, and why therefore the evolution of the capitalist economy towards a point at which revolution was inevitable has not occurred. In this context the Welfare State is seen as providing a package of measures on behalf of capitalism which both increase the efficiency of capitalism and eliminate some of its worst abuses. Towards the first of these ends social security provides benefits which increase the health and efficiency of workers, thereby contributing to the provision of a usable labour force. Social security measures also help to sustain the 'reserve army of labour' of the unemployed, ready and available to come back into the labour force when needed. Contributing to the alleviation of the 'abuses' of capitalism are measures which meet the needs that the capitalist economic system cannot meet, such as provision for individuals in sickness and old age. Such measures reduce dissatisfaction with the capitalist economic system in general, reducing the extent to which it is then threatened by political movements seeking radical or revolutional change. In this way threats to the 'legitimacy' of the capitalist system are reduced.

The last paragraph has, of course, only provided a very simplified statement of what has become a very elaborate approach to the examination of the role of economic power, and its relationship to other forms of power, in the modern capitalist state (see McLennan 1989, for example). The general point being made here is that, whether or not we find Marxist modes of thinking acceptable, this sort of analysis of social security reminds us that the advocates of improved social security policies have to operate in a political context in which the advocates of measures to strengthen and sustain the capitalist economy have powerful voices. The successful advocacy of social security policy changes may well depend upon the extent to which the measures involved procure the approval of these powerful groups, and the extent to which they are seen to be contributing to the goals of these groups.

In the liberal–pluralist approach to the same subject, we of course find echoes of the considerations outlined in the last remarks in the paragraph above. The kind of political analysis undertaken within the liberal–pluralist tradition concerns issues about the strengths of the various influences upon political decision-making. It differs from the neo-Marxist political economy approach in its desire to weight these various influences and in its ultimate belief in the openness of the political system (see Hall, Land, Parker and Webb 1975). By contrast the political economy approach offers a perspective on our subject which is either pessimistic in its conclusions about the feasibility of effective measures to attack inequality or is inviting us to draw conclusions about the need for revolutionary change to transform the economic order. Of course, within the liberal–pluralist tradition we find a range of interpretations of the system, from at one extreme a perspective about the power of the forces sustaining the status quo that is really very close to the neo-Marxist one, to, at the other extreme, a view which sees the system as very open. At the 'open' end of the spectrum we find analyses of the growth of social security policies which suggest that politicians have been willing to expand rapidly the state contribution to welfare, competing with each other in attempting to increase the largesse supplied by the state at the expense of the economy. It is a characteristic of some forms of contemporary 'New Right' thinking to suggest that political processes of this kind have led to an excessive growth of state expenditure on welfare objectives, with damaging consequences to the economy (Buchanan and Tullock 1962; Brittan 1977). Curiously, therefore, some 'New Right' thinkers have developed an analysis of state expenditure on social security and other welfare objectives which is very like that of some of the neo-Marxist writers, in particular James O'Connor (1973), which sees state expenditure as growing dramatically as a response to the dysfunctions of the capitalist economy.

Overall, the political science approach to the analysis of social

security policy offers a significant challenge to those interpretations of the growth of the Welfare State which, drawing upon the
evidence accumulated by scholars in the social administration
tradition, see it as a series of responses to the needs demonstrated
by studies of poverty. They suggest that one cannot simply explain
political responses in these terms, but must instead recognize the
parts played by political pressures and conflicts in producing the
policies we have today.

THE IMPLEMENTATION APPROACH

This final section deals with an approach which is implicitly a part
of the political science approach to the study of social security
policy. It is, however, emphasized here in a separate section
because I regard it as very important to include within an analysis
of social security policy a thorough consideration of many of the
issues about the way policies work in practice. The value of recent
work emphasizing implementation is that it draws attention to the
differences between policy and practice, and that it raises
important questions about the factors that determine this gap (see
Ham and Hill 1984; Hill and Bramley 1986). In social security
policy it is important to recognize that policies are delivered
through complex bureaucratic systems, and that there are many
situations in which 'street-level' staff (Lipsky 1980) are expected
or left to use their own discretion to determine what to do in
practice. There are also situations in which, even without discretionary powers, their actions may mould or distort policy in
practice. These considerations become particularly important
wherever policy goals are ambiguous or alternative policy goals
are in conflict. There are many examples of these phenomena
within social security policy but, in addition, as emphasized in the
introductory section, the whole system is complicated in practice
by the many situations in which social security policy interacts with
other policies with significantly different objectives.

Some work in the tradition described here as the implementation approach, with which I myself have been particularly associated, also emphasizes that there is seldom a clear distinction to be
drawn between policy-making and implementation. It is a false
picture of the policy process to assume that policies are passed

down to implementation staff with their goals and objectives clear, their ambiguities eliminated and their relationships to other policies adequately sorted out.

The implementation approach is important not only for the light it throws upon the working of current policies in practice, but also for the contribution it makes to the examination of the feasibility of alternative policies. It is very important for those advocating policy change to come to terms with the problems entailed in translating policy into action. It is also important to recognize that where specific policies come into conflict with strongly entrenched interests, pressures to change and distort the way those policies work in practice will be particularly strong.

CONCLUSIONS

This brief introductory chapter has sought to give the reader a very general idea of what studying British social security policy entails, and some idea of the alternative schools of thought and approaches upon which the book will have to draw. The book will set out to use all the approaches outlined above, but a distinctive feature of this book arises from my belief that the last two approaches – particularly the implementation approach – have been given less attention in previous writings on social security than they should have. There has been a tendency for writers belonging to either of the first two schools of thought to engage in policy advocacy and the criticism of existing forms of policy, without giving a great deal of attention to issues about the political determinance of policy or issues about the ways in which policies are translated into action. This book aims to redress this balance.

2. The Last Days of the Poor Law

INTRODUCTION

In a book which focuses on contemporary policy and policy-making it is always difficult to decide how much past history to include. Any activities in the present are always at least partly, and often substantially, explicable in terms of past history. Furthermore, it is of course an entirely arbitrary decision which is needed to determine where history stops and the analysis of contemporary events starts. Yesterday's events are history, yet we tend to deal with most recent events in a different way to those in the far distant past. In policy studies there is moreover a tendency to see the contemporary systems as the creation of a specific major piece of legislation. In the case of British social security the legislation which enacted the reforms recommended by Beveridge in the 1940s is often seen in this way. Hence, whilst this book concentrates on events since the Beveridge Report of 1942, it is necessary to precede this with a chapter which sketches in the earlier events in the history of British social security policy.

The British policy debate about social security since the 1940s has been dominated by the Beveridge model. Yet it is important to note that many of the features of that model were established before the 1940s; indeed they were established in the period immediately before the First World War and substantially elaborated in the postwar period. It should also be noted that Beveridge himself was one of the architects of the pre-First World War social security measures. Hence, one of the themes in this chapter will be the early influences upon the National Insurance, or Beveridge, model for social security.

Whilst one of the themes in the history of social security is the development of the National Insurance system, to supersede, for some people, means-tested social security, another theme is the shift from that system of means-tested benefits known as the Poor Law to the development of a national system of means-tested benefits, in which some entitlements are guaranteed and many of the most oppressive features of the Poor Law are absent. For historians of the Poor Law, the reforms of 1834 are an important landmark. It is interesting to note, therefore, that a measure enacted exactly 100 years later, the Unemployment Act of 1934, which created the Unemployment Assistance Board, effectively supplanted the central task of the Poor Law and established an approach towards the provision of means-testing benefits which has been dominant ever since. Whilst the Poor Law was not actually entirely abolished until the National Assistance Act of 1948, the legislation of 1934 effectively took away some of its central functions. With the benefit of hindsight we can say that, because means testing has become very much more important for the British system than Beveridge envisaged it would be, the 1934 Act now stands alongside the National Insurance Act of 1946 as a foundation stone of the modern social security system.

THE NINETEENTH-CENTURY BACKGROUND

The British system of locally administered, and largely locally funded, means-tested relief, the Poor Law, originated in the reign of Queen Elizabeth I. The Elizabethan legislation aimed to keep poor relief to a minimum sufficient to prevent widespread social unrest, and sufficient to facilitate the outlawing of begging. It was a system which was bound to come under strain as British society changed, with the substantial industrialization, accompanying population movements and rural depression which developed in the eighteenth century. The Poor Law reforms of 1834 aimed to reassert the basic Elizabethan principles, whilst adapting the system to an age in which there was a strong commitment to the development of an industrial society and some aspirations towards control over processes of social change. The 1834 Act has been seen as involving a strong commitment to the time-honoured principle of 'less eligibility' – that is, policies to ensure that anyone receiving poor relief should be worse off than the lowest class of paid labour. To make the principle of 'less eligibility' operative, the 'workhouse test' was used. Its aim was to ensure that anyone receiving relief should be required to leave their family and go into the 'workhouse', where a rigorous work regime would be imposed upon them and their standard of living would be maintained at the minimum possible. At its most rigorous the workhouse test involved separating members of families from each other and operating different regimes for different classes of paupers.

Historians of the Poor Law have shown that, in many areas, the principles of 1834 were not fully adopted (Rose 1972). It was costly to establish effectively separate workhouses and in many areas it proved cheaper to continue to be prepared to pay some forms of outdoor relief. The principles of 1834 were based upon the assumption that individuals should be able to support themselves through work, and relief was therefore designed to reinforce commitment to the labour market. Thus, comparatively little attention was given to measures to provide relief for people unable to work. However, as the nineteenth century wore on, it became recognized that there was a group of people whose poverty and inability to work stemmed from chronic sickness and advancing age. This group increased in evidence as standards of health care rose and the chronically sick or disabled were enabled to survive longer. The search for appropriate and economic ways of supporting this group stimulated the development of forms of outdoor relief.

In Chapter 1 reference was made to the important studies, made at the end of the nineteenth century by Booth and Rowntree, of the incidence of poverty. These systematic students of poverty were by no means the only writers to draw attention to the widespread evidence of poverty in the late nineteenth century. Increasingly, attention was given to those manifestations of poverty which might be argued to be threatening to the structure of society. Increasingly, charitable enterprises sought to target their efforts upon a group of people often described as the 'deserving' poor – that is, the group of people who were deemed to be unavoidably poor and making every effort to solve their own problems.

The second half of the nineteenth century also saw the widespread development of forms of 'self-help'. These involved the development of a variety of institutions – the friendly societies, the building societies, trades unions – which had amongst their objectives concerns to work collectively to prevent individuals falling into poverty and being forced to have recourse to the Poor Law. Individual efforts to save, to provide protection against

future misfortunes, were thus supplemented by collective efforts
to support and sustain individual self-help. It was thus possible to
identify the developing importance of a group of people who may
be described as the 'respectable working class'. Industrial and
urban society was throwing up a group of people who were an
important source of skilled and semi-skilled labour, and who
showed signs of wanting to work for the improvement of their
social situations and that of their class. Hence, alongside essentially self-help movements we see the development of political
activities amongst this group of people, involving in particular the
development of trade unionism and then subsequently an interest
in affiliating those organizations to the existing political parties or
in developing new, more working-class-oriented, political movements. The extension of the franchise, bringing many of the males
from these groups into the electorate, obviously also stimulated
political activity. For the already dominant political élites in
nineteenth-century Britain these new movements were seen both
as elements to be mobilized politically and as potential sources of
threat to the status quo (these issues are examined in Gilbert 1966;
Harris 1972; and Thane 1982). We find, therefore, in late
nineteenth-century Britain, both the emergence of socialist-
oriented political movements placing the problems of poverty
centrally on their agenda and a variety of arguments from anti-
socialist élites about how to deal with the phenomena with the
minimum of damage to the existing order. Policies to incorporate
the 'respectable working class' were canvassed, implying, for
social security, state-supported insurance schemes to prevent
destitution. These were seen as building upon, and were therefore
inevitably ultimately heavily influenced by, developing commercial and voluntary insurance schemes. As far as more deprived
groups were concerned, calculations were made about the extent
of danger from the 'urban mob', and about therefore how the
more efficient operation of both charity and poor relief could
eliminate this threat.

We may therefore see concerns about the need for social reform
coming on to the agenda at the end of the nineteenth century,
both as a consequence of increasing evidence about problems of
poverty, poor housing and bad health, and in consequence of the
recognition of the new political forces. To all this may be added
the importance, in this era of emergent nationalism and imperial

adventure worldwide, of concerns about the need for a fit and
unified nation to compete effectively in world affairs. The Boer
War, which occurred just at the turn of the century, provided a
sharp reminder to Britain's political leaders that world dominance
could not be taken for granted. The great British Empire found it
difficult to put down a rebellion from an apparently weak group
of isolated farmers in South Africa, and discovered during the
process of trying to recruit for that effort that large numbers of its
potential working-class volunteers were in poor health and of
inadequate physique.

However, whilst the concern about the condition of the people
played an important part in the social reform movements of this
period, we will find, when we turn to the specific social security
reforms which were enacted, that it would appear to be the desire
to meet some of the aspirations of the 'respectable working class'
which seemed to dominate reform measures.

THE SOCIAL SECURITY MEASURES OF THE 1906–16 LIBERAL GOVERNMENT

The election of the Liberal government in 1906 brought to power
a government committed to social reform measures and which
enacted three important measures for the development of social
security in Britain. These were the Old Age Pensions Act of 1908
and the two measures embraced within the National Insurance Act
of 1911, providing for sickness benefits and for unemployment
benefits for some categories of workers. These reforms need to be
seen very much as measures designed to assist respectable
working-class people to avoid having recourse to the Poor Law.
They were measures very much influenced by nineteenth-century
self-help movements, and by the concerns of the charities. In the
second two of the three measures the central device adopted was
the development of a state-supported system of insurance. This
was an idea that had been gaining ground elsewhere in Europe,
and the British legislators were much influenced by developments
in Germany (Hennock 1987). The first of the measures did not use
the insurance principle, but was nevertheless designed in a way
which was intended to make it an alternative to the Poor Law for
the 'respectable working class'. In view of the importance of these

three measures, we will look at their characteristics in a little more detail.

The Old Age Pensions Act of 1908 provided a modest means-tested pension for people over 70 years of age. As originally designed, people who had received poor relief earlier in their lives were to be disqualified from receiving this benefit. In practice this disqualification proved difficult to operate, and was soon abandoned. However, the significance of this Act lay in its provision of benefits on the basis of a simple means test, thereby moving away from the purely discretionary provisions available under the Poor Law and providing a form of 'outdoor relief' more or less as 'of right'.

The unemployment insurance provided under the 1911 National Insurance Act represented a very significant departure from the attitude towards unemployment which had dominated nineteenth-century economic thinking and had been embodied in the 1834 Poor Law. That attitude had been to regard all unemployment as voluntary, resulting from idleness and the unwillingness of potential workers to offer their labour at the prevailing market price. The concept of unemployment itself would have been meaningless to the founders of the 1834 Poor Law, as it only entered into the political vocabulary in the last part of the nineteenth century, when it began to be recognized that fluctuations in business produced rises and falls in the volume of work available. This led to a recognition that unemployment might not be an entirely voluntary phenomenon, and that individuals might need both help in relocating themselves in work elsewhere and income support during that period of relocation. The unemployment insurance scheme introduced in 1911 was very much a response to this sort of unemployment problem. It was confined to three trades – shipbuilding, engineering and building – where employment prospects were generally good but tended to fluctuate over time. Strict insurance rules were applied – with contributions from employees, employers and the state – and benefits were limited, depending upon past contributions and only available for up to a maximum of a year. Hence, it could be presented as a measure of state-supported self-help, which would not be open to exploitation by potential beneficiaries. Despite this, regulations were included to prevent the payment of benefits to people deemed to have lost their own jobs or found to be making inadequate efforts to get new jobs. It was therefore very much a measure for the involuntary unemployed, those suffering frictional unemployment as a consequence of the trade cycle, and not a measure the benefits of which would extend to the unemployed in general. The scheme did not take into account the fact that there was also a chronically underemployed group amongst the low-skilled and very poor, who still had to seek their help from the punitive and rigorously policed Poor Law system.

The scope of the insurance scheme to provide help for the sick, enacted in 1911, was rather wider and covered all manual workers. But a similar pattern of insurance rules operated to make this also an example of state-supported 'self-help'. The scheme provided for employees, but not for their families, both sickness benefits, if they were out of work as a result of sickness, and medical treatment from a 'panel' doctor. It built upon the already important contribution being made towards the care of the sick by the Friendly Societies and industrial insurance companies, and also involved them in the operation of this part of the National Insurance scheme, giving, in practice, state sustenance to some very shaky ventures.

There is a very important issue about National Insurance which has haunted the evolution of social security, and about which there are many popular misconceptions. Private insurance schemes are, by definition, 'funded' since they will, of course, become bankrupt if the demands upon them exceed either the contributions coming in or balances saved and invested. To protect this funding principle, actuaries are employed to calculate the likelihood that individual contributors will make demands upon the companies, and individual contributions are then determined by the likelihood of such demands. State insurance schemes need not be constrained in this way, and indeed it is generally the case that the state schemes practise 'risk pooling' in such a way as to enable the needs of those particularly likely to make claims upon the schemes to be supported by those less likely to make demands. However, state schemes may go further than that in providing public funds to underwrite the system as a whole. Once it is agreed that this should be done, the state then faces another question: should the scheme be funded as a whole, so that savings are accumulated and contributions are adjusted over time to enable the scheme to remain solvent, or should it adopt the 'pay-as-you-go' principle?

If it adopts the latter, what happens in practice, regardless of the contribution formula, is that current contributions are used to pay current benefits, and the idea of building up a fund over time is abandoned. Political considerations, together with the fact that public expenditure as a whole is managed on a pay-as-you-go basis, incline governments to adopt this principle. In fact, the British National Insurance scheme began as a funded scheme but evolved into a pay-as-you-go scheme very soon after its inception. Governments have continued to maintain the fiction of funding, by providing accounts for a separate National Insurance fund, but in practice budgeting of National Insurance has been essentially on a pay-as-you-go basis. We will see in the next section that it was political pressures for the extension of National Insurance in the years after the First World War which accelerated the demise of the funding principle (Gilbert 1970).

SOCIAL SECURITY IN THE INTERWAR PERIOD

Since the period around the 1911 Act and the period of social reform in the 1940s contained the most dramatic changes to the British social security system, there is a danger of ignoring a number of important events which occurred in the interwar period. This account of that period will deal first with some developments relating to pensions and sickness benefits, second with the complicated story of unemployment relief in the 1920s, third with developments affecting the Poor Law in this period and finally with the significant amalgamation of the issues of both unemployment and the Poor Law in the early 1930s, centring around the Unemployment Act of 1934.

We can deal fairly briefly with the issues about pensions and sickness benefits. There were no significant changes to the system of sickness benefits in the interwar period, although the evolution of the existing scheme during this time was uneven. The scheme, as we have seen, linked sickness benefits with the provision of medical services, administered partly through a range of organizations known as 'Approved Societies'. A very uneven structure of benefits grew up under this scheme, depending upon the viability of individual Approved Societies, so that in effect those with fitter members were able to pay better benefits. Here, then, funding principles still dominated at the expense of equality of treatment.

So far as pensions were concerned, the government came under pressure to extend the 1908 Act. Since this did not use insurance principles, any extension would have considerable public expenditure implications. Therefore, a pay-as-you-go insurance approach offered a temptation to an economy-minded government to extend pension provisions at minimal cost to the Exchequer. New contributions could be used to pay for existing pensioners. Hence in 1925 pensions provisions were developed for workers already contributing to the sickness insurance scheme.

The history of unemployment insurance in the interwar period is very much more complicated. During the First World War the original scheme was slightly extended, but after the war the government came under pressure to extend unemployment benefits extensively to meet the needs of unemployed ex-servicemen, and to fulfil its wartime pledges of better social support in the immediate postwar period. It is also true to say, as historical studies of official records in this period have shown, that the government was panicked into extending unemployment benefits by fear of unrest, or even revolution (Gibert 1970). Thus, an 'out-of-work donation' was brought in very quickly at the end of the war to try to help with the dislocation of labour at that time, and was made available to ex-servicemen and to individuals who had been payers of health insurance contributions. The rates of this benefit, to be christened the 'dole', were fairly high and lasted for up to 26 weeks, hence it was costly to the Exchequer. The measure was followed by the Unemployment Insurance Act of 1920 which extended the 1911 scheme to nearly all manual workers and to most non-manual workers earning less than £250 per year.

After the sharp rise in unemployment immediately following the war, unemployment dropped to quite a low level, but then it jumped dramatically in 1921. The government then found itself committed to high levels of expenditure upon unemployment benefit, and thus began a protracted search for ways of bringing the costs of the scheme under control. Consequently, the unemployment benefit scheme went through a large number of changes, the details of which need not detain us here. However, it is important to note how two kinds of control measures were elaborated in this period (see Deacon 1976). One of these involved the extension of measures designed to prevent claims being made by those who could not prove they were 'genuinely seeking work'.

These measures, initially particularly directed at trying to reduce numbers of married female claimants, led to a range of measures to police the unemployment registers which became notorious during this period. The other control measure was the adoption, within the state scheme, of measures involving forms of means testing. In passing, it is also worth noting what an important role controversy about levels of unemployment benefits played during this period. Indeed, a Cabinet argument about whether or not it was justifiable to cut benefits played a major part in the events leading to the fall of the 1931 Labour government.

Turning now to look at the role of the Poor Law in this period it is not surprising to find, given the developments in the public policy response to the unemployed, that this was in general a period in which 'outdoor relief' was widely extended to all classes of applicants, since it would have been inappropriate to continue to administer the strict 'workhouse test' at a time when other relief measures were multiplying. Nevertheless the shadow of the workhouse still dominated the Poor Law system in this era, as did also the application of what became known as the 'household means test', whereby applicants for poor relief had to disclose details about the means of all members of their households, and had to be prepared to sell possessions and reduce themselves to the lowest levels of destitution before they could get help.

In this time of change it is also not surprising to find resistance on the part of social movements, such as the National Unemployed Workers' Movement, to the strictness of the Poor Law, and increasing numbers of local Poor Law Boards of Guardians who were unwilling to administer the Poor Law in the way that central government required. In the 1920s Boards of Guardians, like the Poplar Board, were pioneers in the provision of generous 'outdoor relief' (Branson 1979). The Poplar Board also came into conflict with central government over the reluctance of the latter to come to the aid of impoverished local areas with high levels of need. The story of the conflict between Poplar and central government is a complicated one; the Poplar Guardians were willing to go to prison in order to draw attention to the unfair treatment of their locality. Their 'extravagant' approach (in the government's terms) to poor relief and its resulting tax and grant implications, operated as a significant pressure towards the centralization of the Poor Law. During the 1920s rules were developed by central government to try to curb the activities of the more generous Boards of Guardians. One of these measures was the Local Government Act of 1929, which replaced the Boards of Guardians by local authority Public Assistance Committees, which were generally bigger than the former Boards of Guardians, being based on the counties and county boroughs. This involved further rationalization of the funding basis for the Poor Law and increased the potential for ministerial control. Nevertheless central concern about the unevenness of local approaches to outdoor relief continued, and in the period after 1929 the Rotherham and County Durham Public Assistance Committees were suspended for being over-generous (Gilbert 1970).

Central government, therefore, saw itself as having two interrelated control problems. So far as the unemployed were concerned, it wanted to accept the general principle of the provision of relief, but wanted to keep expenditure on it under strict control. On the other hand the Poor Law system was operating as a 'safety net' back-up for the unemployment insurance system, and its decentralization posed problems of control for the government. The Unemployment Act of 1934 set out to solve these two problems by providing an Unemployment Assistance Board to administer a national system of means-tested benefits for all the unemployed. This enabled the government to limit the extent to which the Unemployment Insurance Fund was being used for the support of the unemployed, and to curb the activities of the more 'extravagant' Public Assistance Committees.

The initial proposal to implement this scheme involved the setting of benefits which, for many individuals, would be lower than those which they had previously been receiving. This met with a massive protest. In response, the government provided for a two-year 'standstill' period in which individuals could continue to receive benefits at their current levels – a form of 'transitional protection' which has been used with each radical alteration to means-tested benefit systems since that time, with its associated problems of injustice and inevitable administrative difficulties. The government then enacted a set of rules, to operate after the 'standstill', which gave discretionary powers to the Unemployment

Assistance Board and its officials. These enabled local arrangements to be made to mitigate an inflexible rule relating to the
taking into account of rent, additions to benefits where individuals
had to follow special diets, and the provision of single payments
to meet exceptional needs.

The system of national means-tested benefits adopted for the
unemployed under the 1934 Act was subsequently elaborated to
enable means-tested benefits to be extended to pensioners without, or with inadequate, insurance pensions, by legislation enacted
in 1940. It formed the model for the national system of means-
tested benefits, adopted under the National Assistance Act in
1948, to replace the Poor Law. It is also a model for means-tested
benefits which has continued to dominate the British system until
the 1986 Social Security Act brought to an end many of the more
elaborate features of means testing which had characterized the
original government response to the unrest about the initial form
of the 1934 Act. Later chapters will show how some of the issues
about rent rules, special additions to benefits and single payments
have been very central to controversy about means-tested social
security in Britain ever since the 1934 Act.

CONCLUSION

By the Second World War Britons had a social security system in
which a succession of developments in the social insurance field
had extended benefits to manual workers. The sickness, pensions
and insurance schemes were not universal, but did apply to
employed persons in most of the lower- and middle-income
categories. In other words, they were applicable for most manual
workers. Needs of other members of these manual workers'
families were met solely by a system of additions for 'dependants'
added on to the insurance benefits and on to the benefits available
under the Poor Law and Unemployment Assistance Board
schemes.

The incremental character of the growth of the new National
Insurance measures between 1911 and the 1940s had produced a
patchy system in need of rationalization. A number of issues had
not been addressed satisfactorily, amongst which was the issue of
provision for children, on which a pressure group campaign had

built up arguing for a system of family allowances available for the support of children whether or not their parents were dependent on benefit or in work (see Land in Hall, Land, Parker and Webb 1975). Another issue on the agenda, but unresolved, concerned provisions for individuals where sickness or disability was explicitly caused by employment. Here, the existing provision was a mixture of the standard insurance benefit system together with the possibility of additional compensation where employers could be proved to be in some sense responsible for the accident or disease. The more general issue of the special needs of the disabled had not been addressed at all.

We see, therefore, that by the Second World War a quite elaborate social security system had grown up, without a great deal of attention having been given to its underlying principles. A new commitment to social reform engendered by the experiences of the Second World War was to lead to further elaboration of the system.

3. The Beveridge Report

INTRODUCTION

The Beveridge Report – a product of one of the earliest attempts of the wartime coalition government to give consideration to the issues of postwar 'reconstruction' – was published in 1942. It is perhaps remarkable that a report that had so much influence on the postwar period should have been published so early in the Second World War. In fact, it seems likely that the war leaders, including Churchill himself (see Kopsch 1970), were embarrassed by so comprehensive a plan for the postwar period appearing at this time. Beveridge's biographer, José Harris, has shown how Beveridge set out to make a strong personal contribution to forward thinking (Harris 1977). He had worked as a civil servant in the pre-First World War period and had been involved in the creation of the original unemployment insurance scheme, and saw his new recommendations as building upon the system of social insurance which had developed in Britain. At the beginning of the report the achievements of the system of social insurance were reviewed and described in the following terms:

> . . . provision for most of the many varieties of need through interruption of earnings and other causes that may arise in modern industrial communities has already been made in Britain on a scale not surpassed and hardly rivalled in any other country of the world. (Beveridge 1942: para 3, p. 5)

The Report goes on, however, to recognize the extent to which this development had been, in various respects, piecemeal:

> . . . social insurance and allied services, as they exist today, are conducted by a complex of disconnected administrative organs, proceeding on different principles, doing invaluable service but at a cost in money and trouble and anomalous treatment of identical problems for which there is no justification. In a system of social security better on the whole than can be found in almost any other country there are serious deficiencies which call for remedy. (Ibid.: para 3, p. 6)

We therefore find, in the Beveridge Report, a very strong analysis of the way in which a systematic social insurance scheme could be built up, together with a powerful advocacy of the policies necessary to underwrite such an insurance scheme. Beveridge described the road to social reconstruction after the war as involving an attack on five giants – namely 'Want, Disease, Ignorance, Squalor and Idleness'. He saw the recommendations in his report as dealing with the problems of 'Want'. The Beveridge Report still reads as a powerful analysis of the range of policies necessary to produce a comprehensive system of income maintenance. However, there are areas of policy which, even in its own terms, it fails to attack satisfactorily. One of these is the determination of adequate levels of benefit to solve, for all time, the problem Beveridge describes as the problem of 'Want'. Another is the difficulties entailed in developing a level of benefits sufficient to cope with the incidence of widely varying needs and costs between different households. A particularly significant example of this lies in the problem of variable housing costs, discussed at some length in the Report as the problem of 'Rent', but not satisfactorily resolved there. Moreover, the inadequacies of the Beveridge Report appear greater when we try to judge it by present-day standards as opposed to the standards and circumstances of 1942. Beveridge makes assumptions about the character of family life and about the nature of employment – particularly the distribution of employment between men and women, but also the nature of employment in general – which are now very dated. These last considerations are very important when we examine whether or not the Beveridge design is still relevant to our own age.

BEVERIDGE'S PROPOSALS

At its core the Beveridge Report contains a set of recommendations for the setting up of a system of social insurance – that is, a system of insurance in which risks are pooled within the community, so that individuals are able to pay flat-rate contributions and receive flat-rate benefits regardless of the extent to which they are liable to be in need of those benefits. In this sense the concept of social insurance is distinguishable from the principles of private insurance in which actuarial calculations are made to determine contributions rates in relation to predicted risks. Beveridge proposed, along the lines established in 1911, that there should be simple contributions from all workers and from their employers together with a contribution from the state. The only deviations from principles of uniform contributions were designed to take into account:

1. the circumstances of young workers;
2. the peculiar position (at that time) of women in the labour market; and
3. the special circumstances of self-employed people.

Whilst the Report proposed flat-rate benefits, these were to be supplemented by additions for the needs of dependants, with children and wives falling into the category of dependants in most cases. Benefits were to be available to compensate individuals for sickness and unemployment, and to provide for their retirement. The only major deviation from the principle of uniform benefits was a proposal that there should be a special system of higher benefits for those who sustained injuries at work, or illnesses as a result of work. This scheme was designed to replace the scheme for workmen's compensation, which was its predecessor. There was to be a system of maternity grants and a system of widows benefits, with both of these secured on the basis of husbands' contributions. Beveridge also advocated a system of maternity benefits based on women's own contributions, to provide income replacement for women who were confined after a period in the labour market. Finally the insurance scheme also provided for a system of death grants.

Beveridge saw this system of social insurance as providing subsistence-level incomes to deal with the overwhelming majority of the income maintenance problems arising from worklessness, however caused. He did however recognize that there would be circumstances in which it would not be comprehensive, and therefore also suggested that there should be a system of 'social assistance' operating through means tests to provide a safety net to cover needs which social insurance was unable to meet. He described the need for 'assistance' as coming about because of a) certain transitional needs and b) certain categories of people whom the social insurance system could not satisfactorily support. The reason transitional need was seen to be important arose from the fact that Beveridge had proposed that the new system of retirement benefits should be phased in gradually over a period of 20 years, during which individuals would build up entitlements. He identified in the other category of people likely to be in need of 'assistance' individuals who for reasons of sickness were never able to get into the labour market, individuals who temporarily failed to fulfil conditions for benefit (in this category he identified individuals who might be disqualified from getting unemployment benefit through 'refusal of suitable employment' or 'leaving work without just cause'), persons with abnormally high needs in respect of diet or care and 'persons in need through causes not suitable for insurance, e.g., some forms of desertion or separation' (Beveridge 1942: p. 142).

It was proposed that the system of social insurance, together with the system of social assistance, should be administered by a single government department – a Ministry of Social Security.

It is also very important to note that the Report argued that no satisfactory scheme of social security could be devised except on the basis of three assumptions about related policy areas. The first of these was that there should be a system of children's allowances payable whether or not the parents were in receipt of any other benefits. In practice Beveridge advocated that these allowances should be payable for the second and subsequent children where individuals were in work, and only extended to the first child when parents were in receipt of one of the insurance benefits. Second, Beveridge argued that there should be a comprehensive health and rehabilitation service for the prevention and cure of disease and 'restoration of capacity for work available to all members of the community' (Ibid.: p. 158). Third, there should be the maintenance of employment, 'that is to say avoidance of mass unemployment' (Ibid.: p. 163). In practice the Report defined this as an unemployment rate at an average of no more than 8½ per cent. It is important to note that the first of these proposals was adopted and enacted with the Family Allowances Act of 1945. The second proposal can be said to have been adopted and enacted in the establishment of the National Health Service, although there is ground to question the extent to which this offered *comprehensive* services or indeed particularly rehabilitation services and services concerned with the prevention of disease – a separate subject beyond the scope of this book. So far as the issue of the maintenance of employment was concerned, what in fact happened was that between the end of the Second World War and the mid-1970s an unemployment rate was achieved which fell far below Beveridge's 8½ per cent. However, since the mid-1970s the British rate has been generally above the level recommended and taken into account by Beveridge in his proposals for his scheme.

THE ENACTMENT OF THE BEVERIDGE PROPOSALS

It is really quite remarkable to be able to record that Beveridge's recommendations were adopted almost in their entirety. The key pieces of legislation enacting the Beveridge scheme were the National Insurance Act of 1946, the National Insurance (Industrial Injuries) Act of the same year, and the National Assistance Act of 1948. There were only three significant respects in which the proposals adopted departed from the Beveridge design. First, the government rejected Beveridge's proposal that the retirement pension should be brought in gradually over a 20-year period: it made arrangements for individuals who had not previously been contributors to the retirement scheme to qualify very much more quickly than that. However, it looks as if that costly deviation from the Beveridge design had consequences for the levels of benefit set for the system as a whole, placing them rather closer to the subsistence level to be guaranteed by the National Assistance scheme than Beveridge would have wished. Second, the government rejected Beveridge's suggestion that unemployment benefit should be inexhaustible, so long as individuals were prepared (after a period of perhaps six months) to accept any kind of work and be willing to go on periods of training. Instead it set up a scheme in which the maximum period of unemployment benefit entitlement was one year. Third, the government rejected the idea that one agency should run the scheme; it set up a separate National Assistance Board to run the safety net assistance scheme. Fourth, Beveridge's very tentative idea for a system of separation benefits was rejected. This is discussed further below.

THE WEAKNESSES OF THE BEVERIDGE SCHEME

The Beveridge Report's assumption that social insurance should become the main mode of provision for the prevention of 'want' in Britain depended upon the establishment of benefit levels well above those set by the assistance scheme. As has already been suggested, the actual decisions taken in determining levels were not satisfactory in this respect. However, what made them particularly unsatisfactory was that having been set at a comparatively low level they were bound to fail to deal with what Beveridge had described as 'the problem of rent', embodied in the fact that individuals' housing costs varied both between different parts of the country and within each specific area. Moreover, as the Beveridge Report identified, this variation could not be seen simply as a consequence of individual choice and could not therefore be brushed aside with the argument that if individuals chose to house themselves more expensively they must meet that cost from within normal resources. A careful rejection of that argument can be found in the Beveridge Report. Despite this, Beveridge found it impossible to come up with an alternative way of coping with variable rent, arguing that any alternative would leave the system open to exploitation by landlords. However, National Assistance did take actual rent into account, normally in full, so that, for many people, it was the level of rent which determined whether or not their needs would be met by the insurance scheme alone or whether they would need National Assistance, basically in order to cope with their housing costs.

When we come to look at the relevance of the Beveridge scheme for today we also need to look very carefully at the way the scheme dealt with the family. In many respects Beveridge was forward-looking for his time; he was very critical of the way the earlier insurance schemes dealt with benefits for married women and he condemned the census for including married women 'who do not work for money outside their homes among unoccupied persons'. Nevertheless, in his plan he adopted an approach to provisions for married women which has been rendered out-of-date both by modern forms of behaviour and by modern values. The Report argues:

. . . the Plan for Social Security treats married women as a special insurance class of occupied persons and treats man and wife as a team. It makes the standard rate benefit or pension that for a man and a wife, subject to reduction if there is no wife or if there is a wife who is also gainfully occupied. It reserves the description of 'adult dependant' for one who is dependent on an insured person but is not the wife of that person. It treats a man's contributions as made on behalf of himself and his wife, as for a team each of whose partners is equally essential and it gives benefit as for the team. (Beveridge 1942: para 107, p. 49)

Beveridge justified this approach using data from the 1931 census which showed that approximately seven-eighths of all married women were not in paid employment. However, that data disregarded extensive non-insured contract work at home (taking in washing and so on) and it was perhaps absurd to use 1931 data in the very different working world of 1942. Beveridge was prepared to see a situation in which married women did not work for money as 'normal', and to argue that, in the exceptional circumstances in which such women were normally employed, any benefit incomes they received should only be seen as a small addition to the family income. They could be allowed therefore to pay lower contributions, and in practice what was adopted was an option which made it possible for married women to choose not to pay contributions at all. Such an arrangement obviously fits ill with the present-day situation in which nearly half of all married women are economically active, and the evidence on the behaviour of younger women and on the aspirations of women in general suggests that, when economic opportunities allow, that proportion will rise much higher. Beveridge's use of the 'team' analogy was quoted above to illustrate a mode of thinking about family relationships which is regarded as unacceptable to many people today.

That, however, is only one part of the problem about the fit between the Beveridge scheme and our society today. Beveridge's use of the 'team' analogy gives some of the flavour of the way he saw relations between men and women within marriage. Whilst the concept of a 'team' has an egalitarian ring it must be recognized that such language is also used to mask distinctly unequal relationships. In the labour market of Beveridge's era women did not necessarily choose to be non-participants; they were often firmly excluded from competition with men. In some areas of employment, including public employment in particular, married women were explicitly 'barred'. The low participation of women in employment in many areas and occupations was reinforced by cultural and social pressures, having the effect of damping down any challenge to the status quo.

Nor should we assume that Beveridge's team ideas prevailed in the division of income within the family, or in partnerships in control over expenditure decisions. It is, in fact, only very recently that social research has begun to probe into questions about the distribution of resources within the family, producing evidence of marked female disadvantage (see Glendinning and Millar 1987). Overall, contemporary feminists have taught us to be very suspicious about cheerful 'team' assumptions like those used by Beveridge, and have argued that it is more appropriate to raise questions about individual access to opportunities to earn income or receive benefits, regardless of gender or family relationships. From this perspective, therefore, a social security system with both income and means-testing principles firmly linked to the concept of the nuclear family as the benefit unit and the male breadwinner as the normal claimant is far from satisfactory.

Beveridge did however recognize that situations of family break-up posed problems for his scheme. In the more straightforward case of widowhood the benefit system devised was founded upon the contributions of deceased husbands. The Beveridge Report also argued that a benefit could be provided to meet circumstances of family breakdown other than through death. This was presented, however, as an option, and in practice it was an option which was not taken up. Beveridge saw it as problematical that any proposal for benefits to separated or divorced women would have to be set in a context in which there was a legal system which apportioned obligations in relation to the concept of 'fault'. If the husband were at fault for family breakdown, then the husband should have a continuing obligation to maintain. If the wife were at fault, Beveridge believed that there would be a problem about the state adopting a role as the payer of benefit. His firm commitment to the idea of insurance led him to argue that, in this case, the system could not be required to pay out where the insured person was herself responsible for her situation. Quite apart from the fact that we now recognize that the concept of 'fault' offers a rather misleading approach to the

explanation of much marital breakdown, the fundamental difficulty here is the use of the insurance concept where the notion
of benefits as 'contingent' upon individuals being in a particular
situation of need regardless of whether or not it would have been
possible to insure against its occurrence would perhaps be more
appropriate.

However, as we have already seen, these considerations did not
inhibit Beveridge from making provision for separated women
within the National Assistance scheme. Again, we must note the
extent to which there have been changes in both attitudes and
behaviour since Beveridge's day. Marriage breakdown has
become very much more common, as has single parenthood
outside marriage, and our legal framework to deal with issues of
separation and divorce has departed substantially from the concept of fault. So we find that, just as employment of married
women has increased so also have what we may describe as
household or family arrangements in which marriage (as perceived
by Beveridge) is not the norm also become very common. Taken
together, these two trends render irrelevant the social insurance
framework in which, despite Beveridge's arguments to the contrary, women have been regarded as likely to get married and
become the 'dependants' of their husbands.

The fact that both the insurance and the means-tested assistance
schemes operate with the assumptions about marriage characteristic of the Beveridge Report is a source of considerable
weakness in the British income maintenance system to this day.
This weakness is a source of difficulties for many low-income
women, and requires the perpetuation of assumptions about the
character of marital relationships (including relationships which
for social security purposes have to be treated as marriages,
despite the fact that they are not formally such) often greatly out
of line with other aspects of contemporary social relationships.
There are issues here, too, about the extent to which social
security may reinforce or undermine specific behaviour patterns,
and about the extent to which it should do so, to which we will
return.

4. Social Security from the Beveridge Report to 1979

THE BEVERIDGE SCHEME IN OPERATION: A VIEW FROM THE END OF THE 1950s

I have an autobiographical reason for choosing to review the situation with regard to the Beveridge scheme in relation to the end of the 1950s because, in 1959, I went to work for the Ministry of Labour on the administration of unemployment benefit, and in 1960 moved from that job to work in a local office of the National Assistance Board. Inevitably, therefore, I tend to relate events both before and after that date in terms of the system I experienced at that time. However, there are other more rational justifications for reviewing the Beveridge scheme from the viewpoint of the end of the 1950s. After the National Insurance Act of 1946 and the National Assistance Act of 1948 there were no significant changes to the social security system until the National Insurance Act of 1959, which was enacted in response to a growing concern about the inadequacies of the pension scheme, and was set against a background of concern about the cost of that scheme. The Labour opposition had been working on a proposal for a graduated pension scheme to enable pensions to be improved with funds drawn from increased contributions by individuals. The government responded by enacting its own, very limited, version of such a scheme, enabling individuals without any private pension provisions to contribute to a graduated pension scheme through which they would slowly accumulate rather limited enhancements to the basic scheme. At the same time they added a graduated contributions system for all. This was the only respect in which the basic design for social security adopted in the 1940s was elaborated in the 1950s.

However, at the end of the 1950s evidence began to emerge about the inadequacies of the Welfare State, and specifically about the unsatisfactory character of parts of the social security system. A group of academic researchers, working at the London School of Economics (LSE) under the leadership of Professor Richard Titmuss, had become engaged in research which examined the adequacies and inadequacies of British welfare policies. In 1958 a group of young radicals published some essays in a book edited by Norman McKenzie called *Conviction*. Included within this volume were essays on welfare policy by two of the LSE group, Peter Townsend and Brian Abel-Smith. In November 1959 Richard Titmuss himself gave a lecture to the Fabian Society, which was subsequently published, called *The Irresponsible Society* (Titmuss 1960) in which he attacked the government policies of the time and argued that, in various respects, the Conservative governments of the 1950s had allowed the Welfare State to atrophy. Specifically on social security, he said, 'in terms of the relationship of national insurance benefits and allowances to average industrial earnings, most beneficiaries are relatively worse off today than they would have been in 1948' (ibid.). Titmuss and his colleagues drew attention to the evidence that Beveridge's expectation that National Assistance would decline in importance, to become a safety net used by comparatively few people, was not coming about. On the contrary it was growing in importance.

On the other hand, evidence was also emerging about problems of poverty amongst individuals who were not supported by the benefit system. A very influential book, *The Poor and the Poorest*, by Brian Abel-Smith and Peter Townsend published some years later in 1965, drew attention to the numbers of individuals with incomes below the state's 'official poverty line' – that is, the level determined by the National Assistance scales. Significant within this group were the earning poor, and many people amongst the non-earning poor who were unwilling to, or deterred from, claiming National Assistance. The data in this book was derived from official surveys carried out in 1960.

Hence, at this time, a number of issues were being put upon the political agenda, each of which will be dealt with in subsequent sections of this chapter. They are as follows:

1. the case beginning to be made for the elaboration of insurance by means of the development of earnings-related benefits;

2. the development of attempts to tackle the issues about low incomes amongst the working poor, and particularly the issues about social security support for children;
3. developing concern about the way the system of means-tested benefit operated, which took the form, in the 1960s, of the development of campaigns to try to guarantee individual's 'rights' to means-tested benefits;
4. a renewed concern to look at the major problem which had been ducked by Beveridge – namely that of the impact of housing costs upon benefit systems.

It must be realized that all of these developments took place against a background of considerable social change, which was of significance for social security policy. Throughout the 1960s and 1970s the elderly population was growing in size, and this development inevitably raised costs both for the social security system and for other welfare services. In this period, also, we see a substantial growth in the numbers of single-parent families – in most cases female-headed households – as a result primarily of increasing instances of marriage break-up and secondarily of the incidence of childbirth outside marriage. In the second half of our period, and particularly in the late 1970s, we see a growth in unemployment, with the unemployment rate at last beginning to rise from the very low levels, which had become accepted, to reach and then pass the levels that Beveridge identified as threatening to his social security scheme. These three phenomena all provided sources of pressure upon public services and fed into a view, which emerged into political debate in the 1970s, that the Welfare State was making demands for public expenditure which might be regarded as excessive both for the workings of the economy (Bacon and Eltis 1976) and the operation of a democratic political system (Brittan 1977). It is not proposed to discuss these issues further here, although we will return to them later in the book, but they must be recognized as important background facts which influenced the debates about the four issues which have been identified above, and to which we now turn.

THE ELABORATION OF NATIONAL INSURANCE

We have already seen that the National Insurance Act of 1959 added, for some contributors, a modest earnings-related pension. We have also seen that this development seems to have been a response on the part of the Conservative government to a growing advocacy of the case for earnings-related benefit coming from the Labour Party. The Labour Party then came to power in 1964 and the new government set to work to try to develop a more universal 'national superannuation scheme', which would extend a state system of graduated pensions offering benefits comparable in terms of their ratio to past earnings (or, so-called replacement income levels) to private pensions. In practice it moved very slowly on this issue, finding it very difficult to confront the awkward political problem about the relationship between a scheme which would only provide enhanced benefits in the long run and the strong demand for pension improvement in the short run. Ultimately, the 1964–70 Labour government failed to enact the superannuation scheme, and its Conservative successor moved slowly towards a limited scheme which would gradually enhance their earlier earnings-related scheme, passing a new Social Security Act in 1973 which had not yet been implemented when they fell from power (see Ellis 1989). The subsequent Labour government then enacted the Social Security Pensions Act of 1975 which replaced the 1973 Act and provided for an earnings-related superannuation scheme, known as the State Earnings-Related Pension Scheme (SERPS). This measure involved allowing individuals who were already in private schemes adjudged by the government to be adequate to opt out of the state scheme, but provided an enhanced state scheme for all other working people. This was essentially a superannuation scheme in which contributions would determine benefits, with inflation-proofing provided by the government. It also included provision to enable allowances to be made for working women whose periods in employment might be broken by periods of 'family responsibilities'.

It is important to note that the National Superannuation Scheme, whilst it appeared to involve the funding of pensions, was, like the flat-rate scheme upon which it was built, a scheme funded, as far as the government was concerned, on a pay-as-you-go basis. This enabled some improvements to be made to the basic pensions scheme, since at its inception the National Superannuation Scheme involved the government in collecting in very much more than it was paying out. This had the effect of easing pressure on the social security budget in the short run, but provided the long-run threat of a situation in which demands upon the scheme might be seriously out of line with incoming contributions. The alternative, 'funding', would have offered a situation in which governments denied themselves usable revenue in the short run but in due course acquired massive investment funds. This option is seldom on the political agenda anywhere (see, for example, Achenbaum's 1986 discussion of this issue in the United States).

Returning now to the 1960s, whilst the Labour government failed to enact changes to the pension scheme it did introduce, by means of the National Insurance Act of 1966, earnings-related supplements to the flat-rate sickness and unemployment benefit schemes, payable for the first six months of periods of sickness and unemployment. This legislation also extended the system of earnings-related contributions, initially developed in 1959, to replace the flat-rate insurance contributions which had been levied under the original Beveridge scheme. In this way these measures initiated a change to the process of contribution towards social security benefits which made these contributions appear very much more like forms of taxation. Graduated contributions were less regressive than flat-rate contributions, but, largely because of the existence of an upper limit to contributions, were more regressive than income tax. The enactment of earnings-related, short-term benefits had the effect of reducing the likelihood that the temporarily sick and short-term unemployed needed to make an application for National Assistance (in fact, National Assistance was renamed 'supplementary benefit' in the same year). Failure to act on pensions, on the other hand, meant that little was done to reduce the dependence of the elderly upon National Assistance. There were further twists to the story of graduated benefits, to which we will return when we examine developments in the 1980s and contemporary policies.

BENEFITS FOR THE WORKING POOR, SOCIAL SECURITY SUPPORT FOR CHILDREN

As recommended by Beveridge, a family allowances scheme had been enacted in 1945, providing support for the second and subsequent children in families. In the period between the 1940s and the 1960s uprating decisions on benefits in this era of comparatively low inflation were generally made on an ad hoc rather than on the annual review basis with which we have become familiar today. In the case of family allowance upward adjustments were particularly rare, and accordingly the value of the benefit fell substantially. For example, Townsend pointed out:

> . . . the family allowance for the second child remained at 8s. between 1953 and 1960, and the allowance for the third and subsequent children increased from 8s. to only 10s., or by 25 per cent, in a period when average money incomes increased by over 50 per cent. (Townsend 1979: 162–3)

Within the social security schemes, both National Insurance and National Assistance, additions were available to benefits for every child in the family, and in the case of National Assistance the benefits even varied according to the age of the child. Therefore, not only was there an absence of support for families headed by low earners in full-time work, but there was also a very real danger that the incomes of those earners would be below the incomes they might achieve if on benefits. The larger the family the more likely that the families of the working poor would be in poverty. Obviously, the issue of what to do about this problem was politically controversial. It was argued that benefit schemes should not be adopted which implicitly encouraged large families, and accordingly the advocates of improvements in family allowance were at pains to show that these improvements would not have that effect. Another argument, coming from the opponents of improvements in child support benefits, was that the problem of the relationship between earnings and benefits was evidence that the benefit rates were too high. However, the advocates of improved levels of family allowance, many of whom came together in a new pressure group, the Child Poverty Action Group, established in 1965, had some success in pressing their case upon the 1964–70 Labour government. In arguing for this improvement they pointed out that there were tax allowances available in respect of children, and they argued that the universal Family Allowance, extended so as to be available for all children in the family, should be enhanced to replace tax allowances. In the early 1960s this was a particularly potent argument because there were still significant numbers of low earners who paid little or no tax. However, by the time the argument for the replacement of child tax allowances by an improved family allowance received official acceptance, in 1968, the value of the tax exemptions for low earners had fallen so that the value of the tentative shift which occurred from tax allowances to family allowance was substantially undermined (see Banting 1979; McCarthy 1986).

When Labour fell from power in 1970 relatively little had been done to improve the family allowance scheme. It still only started with the second child, and the rates of benefit were still low. The incoming Conservative government produced a Green Paper (HMSO 1972) arguing for a system of 'tax credits' as an alternative approach to the subsidy of the working poor, particularly the working poor with children. This tax credit scheme represented adoption of some of the ideas emerging from the advocates both of 'negative income tax' and 'social credit', involving the idea of guaranteed minimum income for the earning poor and a state benefit which would taper off as earnings rose. It recognized that it would be costly to implement this scheme and that there would be administrative complications about the development of a measure which combined taxation and benefits. Accordingly, as a temporary measure, the government brought in the family income supplement (FIS) scheme, whereby low earners with child dependants were able to apply for a means-tested benefit to supplement their wages. They applied for this benefit to the social security authorities and the government avoided the complicated administrative issues which would have been encountered had the tax authorities been involved. This so-called 'temporary' measure was introduced in 1970 and has remained a significant part of the system of means-tested benefits. Its successor, 'family credit', introduced under the 1986 Act, continues the principle of a separate means-tested benefit for families. The Conservatives have moved no further towards the integration of taxation and benefits.

The introduction of family income supplement was met by

substantial criticism that the government was reintroducing the public subsidy of low wages – the so-called Speenhamland System which had been abolished in 1834. The government's critics argued that effort should have been concentrated upon strengthening the universal benefit, family allowance, rather than upon the introduction of a new means-tested benefit with a comparatively low 'take-up' (Field 1972).

The campaign to strengthen family allowance continued and, with the coming to power of the Labour government in 1974, the 'poverty lobby' had some success, thanks to having persuaded some powerful trade union leaders to 'change sides' on this issue, in persuading the government to rename family allowance 'child benefit', to extend it to the first child, and to accept that it should be regularly uprated in line with inflation. This was a costly commitment, and just before its enactment there were signs that the government might renege on the deal (see McCarthy 1986: ch. 11). The 'poverty lobby' leaked confidential Cabinet papers to the press and succeeded in securing substantial trade union support for a campaign to prevent the government going back on its word.

Hence, by the end of the 1970s the structure of support for the working poor consisted both of an improved child benefit and of the means-tested family income supplement. It also included a system of rebates available for rents and rates – a topic to which we will return in the section after next.

THE OPERATION OF MEANS TESTING: THE DEVELOPMENT OF WELFARE RIGHTS

With the recognition, in the early 1960s, that National Assistance was growing rather than declining in importance in the social security system, the proponents of measures to improve the income maintenance system began to develop a two-pronged strategy. This is, of course, an oversimplification of the situation since, for some individuals, one prong of the strategy was very much more important than the other, and to some degree the adoption by specific individuals of the two-pronged strategy involved a danger of the advocacy of contradictory policies. The two-pronged strategy involved, first, arguing for the strengthening (by means of regular uprating and introduction of earnings-related supplements) of the National Insurance benefits and, second, the development of the National Assistance scheme in such a way that individual entitlement to benefit would be very much more explicit. National Assistance was seen as the heir to the Poor Law, accordingly carrying with it some of the stigma of the earlier system. It was regarded as important that individuals, despite having to undergo a means test, should have a *right* to this benefit if their income was low. It was felt that there was a need to change the image of National Assistance, to write the regulations in a way which made entitlement clear, and to minimize the areas of decision-making which were subject to the unregulated discretion of individual local officials. The first move in this direction was the 1966 Ministry of Social Security Act which created a unified income maintenance ministry to take responsibility for both National Insurance and means-tested benefits. The National Assistance Board was abolished and replaced by the Supplementary Benefits Commission, which was to operate as an advisory body to the Ministry and as the body responsible for the administration of the discretionary elements in the means-tested benefit scheme. The scheme itself was then renamed Supplementary Benefit. The powers to use discretion to reduce benefits were limited: benefits for the elderly could not be reduced, but discretion might be used to increase them, whilst the circumstances in which benefits for younger claimants could be reduced were quite closely circumscribed. An attempt was made to reduce the extent to which individual benefits were enhanced by discretionary additions, replacing such additions by higher basic benefits; this later proved to be comparatively unsuccessful.

We have already noted the growth of pressure group activity around social security issues in this period. This activity soon began to concern itself not merely with policy advocacy but also with trying to help individuals to make claims for benefits. Soon after its inception, the Child Poverty Action Group developed a strand of activity which involved producing publications which gave information on benefits, and giving aid and advice to individual claimants. Pressure groups, local voluntary organizations, and sometimes organizations of claimants themselves, began to engage in what are now described as 'welfare rights' activities on behalf of individual claimants. A movement began to be identifiable, growing out of the longer-standing aid and advice activities of bodies like Citizens Advice Bureaux, and drawing ideas from rights movements in the United States (see MacGregor 1981; Fimister 1986).

This welfare rights activity developed a number of tactics to try to deal with problems about means testing. Campaigns were developed to encourage individuals to take up benefits, individuals were assisted in making applications and in appealing against decisions. The new Supplementary Benefits Commission became the subject of very thorough day-to-day scrutiny by this emergent movement. There developed an extensive critique of discretion within the supplementary benefit scheme. This discretion occurred in two interrelated forms. First, the legislation gave the Supplementary Benefits Commission itself the power to elaborate internal working rules to guide everyday decision-making. This was the phenomenon Bull has called 'agency discretion' (Bull 1980), the main manifestation of which was a series of secret rule books known as 'codes', in which local officials were provided with instructions on how they should exercise day-to-day decision-making powers in respect of individual claims. The welfare rights movement argued that the secret rule books should be made public, and should be embodied in either primary legislation or secondary legislation (regulations) which could be challenged in the courts and in tribunals. This would imply the development of the existing appeal arrangements into a system which could establish formal precedents. To help to push the system in this direction the welfare rights movement acquired leaked copies of the 'codes', and provided advice on how to challenge decision-making based upon them.

Second, even within the Supplementary Benefit Commission-interpreted law there were a variety of situations in which local staff were effectively required to exercise their discretion to determine payments. The internal guidance on this varied from, at one extreme, elaborate instructions which merely left officials to determine whether people fitted carefully predetermined categories, to, at the other extreme, very open-ended advice which left the officials free to use discretion to commit resources in unanticipated 'exceptional' circumstances. Some writers on the phenomenon of discretion (notably Donnison 1982: 83–4) have described the former as judgement, the latter as discretion. Whilst recognizing that qualitatively different issues arise if discretion is relatively unstructured than if it is subject to considerable predetermination, it is the view here that this judgement–discretion distinction is not a particularly useful one. However, as already said, the concern of the welfare rights movement was both to bring the instructions relating to the former into the public arena where they could be subject to legal argument and to minimize the extent to which very wide discretionary powers were allowed. In the pursuit of the latter goal they of course encountered something of a dilemma, very well demonstrated in an article by Titmuss (1971), that, whilst they wanted clearer rules they did not want restrictive rules which rendered the system less generous. Since, in practice, discretion is peculiarly difficult to eliminate, particularly in those forms which are at the judgement end of the spectrum (to use Donnison's distinction) this will be shown, in later discussions in this book, to have been a persistent problem for the welfare rights movement. By contrast, we will see that the elimination of 'agency discretion' was relatively easily achieved, but may, in long-term retrospect, have been a Pyrrhic victory for welfare rights.

At the end of the 1960s the Supplementary Benefits Commission – led at that time by an academic who had been very close to Richard Titmuss and his colleagues at the London School of Economics, David Donnison – persuaded the government to undertake a full review of the supplementary benefit system with a view to developing a much clearer rule structure. The recommendations from this process of review were published shortly before the fall of the Labour government in 1979 (DHSS 1978). In publishing them, the government stressed that the resources available for social security reform were limited and that there was a need to concentrate reform of supplementary benefit upon the clarification of the rule structure. This decision very clearly exposed the divisions within the campaign for reform between the case for universal, National Insurance-based, benefits which would eliminate the need for means-tested benefits and the elaboration of the means test structure. Government spokespersons, and to an extent David Donnison himself, urged critics to come to terms with the fact that the system of means-tested benefits was of fundamental importance for the protection of the incomes of the poor. They argued the case for the reform of this system, and therefore to some extent the acceptance of the centrality of this system for the relief of poverty. The critics continued to argue for a reaffirmation of the Beveridge ideals (Lister 1979; Parker 1989). Before any actions could be taken to enact the proposals set out in the review of supplementary benefit the Labour government fell. In fact, many of the proposals of the review were adopted by the incoming Conservative administration, but that story belongs to Chapter 5.

HOUSING AND SOCIAL SECURITY

In order to put a discussion of housing and social security into context, it is necessary to remember (as was stressed in Chapter 1) that there are a variety of ways in which the state contributes towards the housing costs of individuals, thereby relieving them from the necessity to pay the full economic cost of their housing. Whilst only some of these ways interact significantly with the social security system, any questions about the form of the system of support for housing costs needs to take into account both those measures which do, and those measures which do not, do so. The major difference is between measures which operate as kinds of universal subsidies to specific groups of people and measures which are specifically targeted by way of means testing. Measures which subsidize housing, without significantly interacting with means testing are:

1. the support of individual mortgage payments by way of income tax relief;
2. the general subsidy of local authorities or housing associations to enable them to provide low-cost housing; and
3. state measures which have the effect of requiring landlords to 'subsidize' tenants by preventing them from charging full economic rents.

Until the 1960s the measures described above were the principal ways in which the state provided help with individuals' housing costs. However, from the 1930s onwards, there had been a number of local experiments concerned with the targeting of the state subsidies to local authority house rents by means of rebate, or differential rent, schemes. A number of local authorities developed schemes, involving on the whole simple forms of means testing, which enabled them to take into account individual incomes in determining individual rent levels. The 1964–70 Labour government, led by Harold Wilson, encouraged local authorities to consider the development of schemes of this kind. In 1966 local authorities were told in a White Paper *Prices and Incomes Standstill: Period of Severe Restraint* that they should adopt rebate schemes if they were forced to raise rents, and in 1967 a Ministry of Housing circular included a recommended rent rebate scheme.

Then, in the early 1970s, the incoming Conservative government took this a stage further. In the Housing Finance Act of 1972 the government developed a new system for central subsidy towards local authority rents which required general rent levels to be moved sharply upwards towards economic rent levels and aimed at the gradual elimination of the central subsidy. In this measure was the idea that subsidies for local authority rents should ultimately be confined to individual means-tested rent rebates. The government provided a national rent rebate scheme, substantially but not wholly subsidized by central government, which was mandatory upon local authorities.

The introduction of a national rent rebate scheme for local authorities brought to a head the problem of the relationship between rent support within the supplementary benefit scheme and rent support by way of the rent rebate scheme. Government needed to work out a way of determining which of these two systems should support the rents of individuals who qualified for supplementary benefit. Such a resolution was needed to prevent situations arising in which either the local authorities or the Supplementary Benefits Commission would become involved in trying to shift responsibility, and accordingly costs, on to each other. It was also necessary so that individual claimants would know where they stood under the two systems. In practice this was difficult to do and a number of anomalies arose. In particular, there emerged what was described as the 'better off problem' whereby some recipients of supplementary benefit would really be better off without that support but getting full rebates, and conversely some recipients of rebates not qualifying for supplementary benefit would be better off paying full rents but receiving supplementary benefit. This arose from the operation of different means-testing principles in the two schemes. The official review of the supplementary benefit scheme, in the late 1970s, identified this as a problem in need of solution, but was unable to come up with an answer.

The Conservative government, elected in 1970, also provided a system of state assistance to private-sector tenants organized along the same lines as the rent rebate scheme. This scheme was known as the rent allowance scheme. The issues arising in connection with this are very similar to those described above with regard to the rent rebate scheme. However, rent allowances enabled individuals to pay rents to private landlords and came therefore in the form of cash payments rather than rebates. The problems this scheme posed also included the danger that state subsidy of private rent-payers would enable private landlords to secure, indirectly, subsidies from the state. The rule structure for the scheme in its early days largely prevented this problem arising, but we will see later that it did become a problem in the 1980s.

Finally, this pattern of means-tested assistance to enable individuals to meet housing costs was further complicated, in this case as far back as 1966, by the introduction of a system of rate rebates. Rates were the system of local taxation, based upon property values, now being superseded by the community charge or poll tax. Whilst the tax on property values was to some degree progressive, inasmuch as better-off people had larger and better houses, it was nevertheless progressive in a very inexact way, and did tend to impose heavy costs upon low-income householders. It was for this reason that the government adopted the rate rebate scheme. This scheme operated with rules which were quite like those brought together in the 1970s for the operation of the national rent rebate and rent allowance schemes. We need do little more here than note that the existence of this benefit, normally paid alongside a rent rebate or a rent allowance, but also paid to low-income house owners, added to the complexity of the interaction between housing support by way of supplementary benefit and housing support by way of locally administered rebates and allowances.

This is all that needs to be said here about developments in support for housing costs in the period between Beveridge and 1979. In the discussion of the Beveridge scheme the problem of housing costs was identified. In the period after the enactment of the Beveridge scheme the initial response to that problem was to provide for the meeting of housing costs through the National Assistance/supplementary benefit scheme, with a consequent significant impact upon the importance of that scheme for income maintenance. Then, in the 1960s and 1970s, the development of an alternative approach to housing cost support, by way of the local authority-administered benefits, seemed to offer a satisfactory alternative to housing cost subsidy by way of the national means-tested scheme. However, in practice it engendered a series of complicated interactions between the alternative local and central housing support schemes. It is noted that the Supplementary Benefit Review (Department of Health and Social Security 1978) identified the need for attention to that problem. A solution emerged in the 1980s which, whilst in some respects simplifying the problem, in other respects added another layer of difficulties. We will give more attention to that issue in the next chapter.

THE POLITICS OF THE 1960s AND 1970s: TRYING TO BUILD ON THE BEVERIDGE DESIGN

This chapter has described how, at the end of the 1950s, discontent built up about the problems of poverty which the Beveridge design for social security failed to prevent. Over the 1960s and 1970s, therefore, attempts were made to elaborate the Beveridge design. At the same time new problems were arising which made it more difficult to ensure satisfactory coverage for insurance benefit.

In terms of the approaches to the analysis of social security outlined in Chapter 1, the 1960s and 1970s may be seen as the hey-day of the social administration approach. A number of studies were completed demonstrating the inadequacies of existing policies (Abel-Smith and Townsend 1965; Townsend 1979). New pressure groups were formed (in particular the Child Poverty Action Group) to draw attention to the issues, and periods of Labour rule in 1964–70 and 1974–79 gave the social administration 'constituency' reasonable access to government. The main achievements of this 'movement' were the introduction of earnings-related benefit, the transformation of the limited family allowance scheme into a potentially more comprehensive child benefit scheme, and some strengthening of 'rights' to means-tested benefit. Yet the gains to actual benefit rates, for those not qualifying for earnings-related benefit, were slight: child benefit by no means covered the cost of children; and social and economic changes independent of social security developments, notably rising unemployment and increases in the number of single-parent households (generally female headed), frustrated the objective of seeing means-tested benefits decline in importance.

In this period, therefore, the increasing cost of social security tended to limit government willingness to concede the comprehensive reforms demanded by those who sought to build on the Beveridge model. Cost considerations continually tempted governments to use 'selective' rather than 'universal' benefits to solve newly emergent problems – rent and rate rebates, the subsidy of lower wages through family income supplements, and extensions of supplementary benefit to single-parent families. Hence, whilst this era was the high point for the 'social administration approach', governments were increasingly ready to listen to alternatives, in which economic arguments about efficiency were salient. Means testing grew, despite Labour suspicions of the device, and in the interlude of Conservative rule – the Heath government of 1970–74 – advocates of more generalized means-testing systems – negative income tax or social credits – received some attention. Whilst the Heath government's contributions to social security policy were essentially ad hoc extensions of means testing – the housing measures in the Housing Finance Act, and family income supplement – their Tax Credit Green Paper flirted with the idea of grander designs.

The politics of social security throughout this period seemed to be dominated by pressure group efforts to further the social administration approach (see McCarthy 1986), but the groups concerned were always weak and likely to be outweighed by arguments from the advocates of public sector economy. In the second period of Labour rule this problem was recognized by such groups as the Child Poverty Action Group, which made strenuous efforts to link up with the trade unions. The idea of a 'social wage' surfaced in Labour Party and trade union thinking on incomes policy in the mid-1970s, only to be eclipsed by economic problems and the collapse of the always fragile incomes policy consensus. By the end of the period of Labour rule, David Donnison

(Donnison 1979) was urging the social administration constituency to come to terms with the harsher social realities of the era. This implied more limited opportunities for social security reform which, from Donnison's perspective as Chairman of the Supplementary Benefits Commission, meant attention to creating a more liberal 'rights-orientated' means-testing system. This approach involved, in many respects, shifting attention from grand questions of policy design to the development of policies whose implementation could be more effectively controlled. It attempted to split off the 'welfare rights' preoccupation of the anti-poverty movement from its 'forward from Beveridge' concern, meeting some of the demands of the former but none of the latter. It was strongly resisted by the pressure groups (see the account in Walker 1983, or publications from the groups, such as Lister 1979). However, while the argument was proceeding the Labour Party lost power, and a very different era for social security began with the election of Mrs Thatcher's Conservative government.

5. From 1979 to 1989

INTRODUCTION

In an account of the history of public policy one inevitably gets into difficulties as one nears the present era, if, as is the case in this book, there is an intention to provide a full account of contemporary policy in the chapter to follow the historical chapters. Hence, this account of the impact of the years of Mrs Thatcher's Conservative government upon social security policy will be rather shorter than might have been expected, given that it was a period of intense policy activity, because in many cases the description of the outcome of this activity can be left to the next chapter in which the policies of the present day will be described.

It was noted in the last chapter that, by the end of the 1970s, a conflict seemed to be building up between the arguments for building upon the Beveridge design and the arguments for rationalizing and extending means testing. The supplementary benefit system had been reviewed, and a set of changes had been recommended. Perhaps, even more importantly, it had been recognized that the problem of housing support for low-income people needed attention in the light of growing contradictions in the system. It is therefore not surprising to find continuation of policy development in social security in the 1980s. However, in addition to this, several reasons may be identified for expecting the Thatcher years to have been a significant period of change for the social security system. Three such reasons may be highlighted.

The first of these reasons is that the Thatcher government came to power committed to cutting public expenditure. It was inevitable, therefore, that it should have to give attention to social security expenditure, forming as it does nearly one-third of all public expenditure. But it is not merely the size of the social security budget which is relevant, but also its rate of growth. In practice, despite sustained efforts to cut social security provisions, the Thatcher government found that social security expenditure continued to rise at a rate well in excess of the growth of any other element in public expenditure. We therefore find the paradox that, between 1979–89, a considerable number of cuts were made to the social security system, with the consequence that the deal it offered to claimants, or would-be claimants, markedly deteriorated, whilst at the same time overall public expenditure on social security grew rapidly. We may identify two major sources of the growth of this expenditure. One of these was an element outside government control, a steady increase in this period of the numbers of people over pension age. The other major source of growth may be argued to be rather more open to government control – namely the growth in the incidence of unemployment which rose substantially in the early years of the Thatcher era, and only fell away slightly from the high levels sustained by 1983 in the late 1980s. To them may be added another source of growth, the responsibility for which can also be laid at the feet of government – the tendency, already noted in the 1960s and 1970s, for the subsidy of the housing of low-income people to be increasingly shifted from subsidy through the housing budget (the subsidy of council housing) to subsidy through the social security system (rebates for individuals).

The second reason why social security secured attention from the Thatcher government was quite closely related to the first. The government came to power committed not merely to the reduction in public expenditure but also to 'rolling back the state'. It was eager to curb the numbers of civil servants and impose strict managerial controls over their activities. The social security system was, and is, quite the largest employer of non-industrial civil servants in Britain. Therefore, quite apart from any concerns about the cost of the social security system in general, the government was bound to be concerned about the cost of its administration. It was therefore very ready to continue the process, initiated by the Supplementary Benefit Review of the 1970s, of seeking for ways of simplifying and streamlining the administration. Again, we face a slight paradox here, for we will see that efforts to confine social security expenditure inevitably led the government in the direction of wanting to replace universal or insurance benefits by means-tested benefits, although means testing is an expensive process in administrative terms. Hence we also find in this period a search for ways to simplify means testing.

The third reason why social security was high on the Thatcherite agenda can be found in the ideology of the New Right. The Thatcher government was not merely concerned to cut back the role of the state because of its cost, it also was, and is, committed to reducing the role of the state in the lives of individuals, strengthening the operation of free markets, and stimulating self-reliance on the part of citizens. Implicit in this ideological position is hostility to the role of social security in protecting individuals from the pressures of the free market.

One way in which the concern to cut public expenditure and the concern to reduce the role of the state were brought together by the Thatcher government was in the desire to replace public provisions by private provisions. The manifestations of this in social security policy were the delegation of responsibility for initial assistance to employees who became sick or pregnant to employers and the encouragement of private pension schemes. However, both of these developments had to be underwritten by extensive amounts of public money.

In the writings of the ideologues of the New Right (Friedman 1962, Harris and Seldon 1979) we find a sustained attack on the idea of the Welfare State. So far as social security is concerned, these writers emphasize an argument for keeping benefits to a minimal level, so that they serve only to prevent the more extreme cases of destitution and operate in such a way that they enforce labour market participation. It is from this school of thought that we find 'negative income tax', involving the use of the tax collection system also as a benefit delivery system for low-income people (see fuller discussion on pp. 157–62), advocated as the ideal approach to social security provision. The shift from the social security system we have today to a system of negative income tax would involve complex administrative change. In particular, it would involve a change, to which there is great civil service resistance, involving the integration of the tax collection system with the benefit delivery system. Thus, in practice, the politicians of the Thatcher era can be said only to have edged our system slowly in the direction of negative income tax. For them, the slogan of the era has been 'targeting'. In other words, they have been committed to decreasing the role played by universal and contributory benefits and increasing the role of means testing in the social security system. Some of the changes, particularly those embodied in the 1986 Social Security Act, do involve some attention to the relationship between the tax system and the benefit system, but the system still remains a long way away from negative income tax.

The actual story of policy change, between 1979–89, consists of a flurry of early measures, including the enactment of changes largely foreshadowed by the Supplementary Benefit Review (Department of Social Security 1978) carried out under the Labour administration, followed by a rather more sustained review of the system in the mid-1980s. The latter was the review of the social security system commissioned by the Secretary of State, Norman Fowler (HMSO 1985), which was presented at the time as the most fundamental review of the social security system since Beveridge. In practice, it concentrated on the means-tested part of the system, and in many respects involved a second go at the issues that had been considered by the Supplementary Benefit Review. Fowler's claim to have engaged in a fundamental review of the system should thus be received sceptically. However, seen in the context of the Thatcher changes as a whole, and in particular the weakening of contributory benefits, this radical attempt to restructure means-tested benefits was an important statement of an alternative philosophy for the administration of social security to that embodied in the Beveridge ideals. The Fowler proposals were embodied in the 1986 Social Security Act which was brought into full implementation in 1988, so the year 1988 is, if not a year of fundamental change comparable to 1946, at least a very important turning-point in the history of the British social security system. This is a point to which we will return at the end of this chapter.

The rest of this discussion of this period will be divided into three sections. The first of these will be concerned with the general efforts to curb social security costs; the second will deal with the various attacks on National Insurance; and the third, final, and longest, section will look at the two bites at the reform of means-tested benefits, the first occurring together in the Social Security Act of 1980 and the Social Security and Housing Benefit Act of 1982, the second being the Social Security Act of 1986.

GENERAL EFFORTS TO CURB SOCIAL SECURITY COSTS: 1979–89

By 1979 a system for the annual review of benefits had been established, which resulted in the uprating of the insurance benefits in line with either the rise in prices or the rise in wages, whichever was greater. At the same time it was generally accepted that the means-tested benefit rates would move in line with these movements in the insurance benefits. In addition, the new system of child benefit operated with similar uprating assumptions. The incoming Conservative government, in one of the two Social Security Acts passed in 1980, explicitly severed the link between uprating and the movement of wages, confining it in future only to the movement in prices. Developments in the early 1980s were more complicated than this, but the general thrust of policy was to try to keep uprating amounts to a minimum through changes in the technique to be used. Ogus and Barendt summarize all this as a determination to impair the 'efficacy' of the previous obligations to maintain the value of benefits involving, alongside the ending of the link with earnings:

> . . . an up-rating of short term benefits for 1980–81 at 5 per cent *less* than the increase in prices (though the cut was later restored when the benefits became taxable); postponement by two weeks of the coming into force of the up-rating order; release from the obligation to maintain the value of the earnings limit placed on retirement pensioners and the dependants of beneficiaries. (Ogus and Barendt 1988: 379–80)

At the same time, both in 1980 and in later changes, there was a tendency for the value of the means-tested benefits, which were in any case only linked to the insurance benefits by convention, to be eroded. Hidden in the 1988 changes, of which more will be said later, was a considerable number of changes which reduced the value of means-tested benefits. Finally, and in some respects as we shall see later most importantly of all, the government refused to continue the process of automatically uprating child benefit. The explicit decisions it took on this issue led to a fall in the relative value of child benefit over the period.

It is also important to note amongst efforts to cut costs, a variety of policy changes which had the effect of denying benefits to specific groups of people. Amongst those who experienced this attack were, most importantly of all, the young unemployed most of whom were required to be on Youth Training Schemes in order to receive any form of state assistance. However, as will be shown later, the rights of all unemployed people to benefits have been significantly limited. There were also measures to limit the availability of benefit to individuals who had taken early retirement, and to married female participants in the labour market. Some of the changes to be described in the next section must also be seen in terms of their contribution to the cutting of social security costs. We will now move on to these.

THE ATTACK ON NATIONAL INSURANCE

There were three quite explicit ways in which the National Insurance system was attacked by the Thatcher government. First, in 1982 (under an Act passed in 1980) the earnings-related additions to sickness and unemployment benefit were abolished. This meant that, whilst the contribution system remained graduated, the benefit system in respect of short-term benefits was restored to a flat-rate system. Second, the system of sickness benefit was replaced by a system of 'statutory sick pay' under the Social Security and Housing Benefit Act of 1982. This involved a requirement for employers to pay sick pay to their employees up to a minimum standard laid down by the state. They are reimbursed for the cost of this responsibility by being allowed a rebate of employers' National Insurance contributions. The 1986 Social Security Act adopted a similar principle for statutory maternity pay. These two measures did not entirely abolish sickness benefit and maternity benefit; these benefits remain for that small group of people who, whilst having been recent National Insurance contributors, are not actually in employment at the point at which they become sick or entitled to maternity benefit. Statutory sick pay only lasts for six months, after which the National Insurance-based invalidity benefit is still available. What is important about both of these measures is the adoption of a new approach to social security administration in which employers can be described as being required to be the agents of government, paying benefits and being reimbursed by contribution rebates.

The Fowler reviews of social security gave considerable attention to the State Earnings-Related Pension Scheme (SERPS). It appeared at one time that entitlement to this benefit might be severely curtailed, but in the end what was enacted was a modification which will ultimately reduce the value of SERPS to individual claimants. In weakening SERPS the government also sought to increase the incentives for individuals to move into private pension schemes. The Fowler review made a great deal of the future cost of SERPS to taxpayers and contributors once there are large numbers of people with full entitlements sometime in the next century. However, ironically, measures to encourage people to contract out of SERPS will have the effect of reducing the contributions coming in to fund current pensions. It seems likely that this deterred radical reform to the SERPS scheme, practical politicians putting aside their concerns about future public expenditure problems in favour of current ones. More will be included on the specific details of the changed SERPS scheme in the next chapter.

In general terms the changes to National Insurance tended to undermine the underlying philosophy of that scheme, which involves individuals making contributions when in work in the clear expectation of benefits if they fall out of work. It is perhaps significant to note that, in the budget of 1988, the Chancellor formally abandoned the principle of Treasury contributions to the National Insurance fund. In many respects the National Insurance fund had always been a symbolic entity; British public expenditure planning did not involve treating this fund as distinctly separate and protected. However, the formal ending of contributions to the fund was yet another sign of the government's view that National Insurance was losing its centrality in the social security system.

MEANS TEST REFORM

As stated above, the Thatcher governments made two distinct sets of changes to the system of means-tested benefits, the first of these being the Social Security Act of 1980 and the Social Security and Housing Benefit Act of 1982 and the second being the Act inspired by the Fowler reviews, the Social Security Act of 1986. We may also distinguish between the reform issues concerned with the main income maintenance benefits and the reforms relating to the system of housing costs. In this section we will deal first with the main income maintenance benefits and then with housing benefit.

As has already been stated, the incoming Thatcher government took on board the case for the reform of the supplementary benefit system as set out in the review report which had been presented to the Labour government (DHSS 1978). This involved some, fairly marginal, simplification of the rules relating to entitlement to supplementary benefit, together with extensive codification of the discretionary powers. In the quest for public expenditure savings, certain of the more generous provisions in the original review proposals were left out, in particular a proposal that, in place of discretionary benefits available for such items as clothing replacements, individuals should get regular lump sum payments to enable them to deal with 'lumpy needs' (see Walker 1983). New rules relating to additional payments to the basic benefits were more restrictive, with grants for clothing replacement largely eliminated. The initial effect of this change was a marked reduction in single payments to supplementary benefit claimants. It looked, for a year or so, as if the new system had succeeded in reducing both the costs of these additional payments and the extensive demands made upon the administration by individual applications for help. However, this short-term gain for the system proved to be illusory since, after about a year, claimants and their advisors learnt how to extract help from the system by using the structure of rules clarifying entitlement, and the demand for single payments rose sharply. This experience was important, influencing the government's decision in the mid-1980s to undertake a further review of the system. That review, the Fowler review, brought forward a very much more radical simplification of the supplementary benefit system.

The new scheme, enacted in the 1986 Act, renamed supplementary benefit 'income support'. It introduced a structure which discriminated very much less elaborately between different categories of claimants, replacing specific additions to individuals' weekly benefits by a uniform structure of premiums, taking into account, for example, whether individuals were disabled or pensioners or the heads of single-parent families. This system will be described in much more detail in the next chapter. The 1986 Act also abolished entitlements to single payments, except in the special cases of help for maternity needs and funerals (although in this case the benefits were limited and replaced the universal National Insurance-related maternity and death grants). The system of entitlement to single payments was replaced by a discretionary Social Fund, providing most of its help (70 per cent) through loans reclaimable from weekly benefits. The 1980 reform may perhaps, with the benefit of hindsight, be described as a victory for welfare rights. Whilst it did involve the elimination of some kinds of discretionary payments it did enshrine in regulations rights to many others. In contrast, the 1986 Act can therefore be seen as a backlash against that victory, with rights to additional single payments largely eliminated. The success of welfare rights 'take-up' campaigns in exploiting the loopholes in the 1980 Act might well have contributed to this subsequent backlash.

In the discussion of policy developments in the 1960s and 1970s, in Chapter 4, some attention was given to the problems of benefits for the working poor. It was noted that family income supplement was introduced in the 1970s, and was seen at that time as a temporary measure preceding the development of a 'tax credit' scheme. That development never occurred, and the continued operation of family income supplement with a means test structure quite different from any other benefit, was a source of problems for the social security system. The 1986 Social Security Act replaced family income supplement by family credit, and in so doing developed for this benefit a means test rather more compatible with that used for income support and for housing benefit. In other words, it created a situation in which the working poor could expect to get a benefit which, if they had children, would sustain them at an income above the income support level. In this way the government tackled a problem which it described as the 'unemployment trap' (see further discussion in Chapter 7) under which it had been possible for individuals to be deterred from taking work by the fact that their income situation would be worse than if they remained on benefit.

The story of means-tested housing support in the 1980s is one of a hasty legislative decision (in 1982) leading on to the urgent need for second thoughts, with this being embodied in the 1986 Act. In 1982 the government developed what they called 'housing benefit', bringing together some aspects of the support housing costs of supplementary benefit claimants with the rent and rebate schemes and the rent allowance scheme. Its aim was to eliminate the anomalies about the existence of the various means-tested housing support schemes operating side by side. In practice the 1982 Act was a 'botched' attempt to do this: some of the anomalies of the previous system were eliminated, but new ones were created (Hill 1984). A special benefit, housing benefit supplement, had to be devised, involving substantial administrative complications.

Overall, the housing benefit system was based upon two quite distinct principles, one deriving from the old local authority rebate and allowances schemes, the other deriving from the supplementary benefit scheme. The hasty enactment of this change seems to have been attributable to a desire to reduce civil service numbers by shifting part of the responsibility for supplementary benefit administration – that is, the part concerned with the assessment of rent support – from the central civil service to local government.

Once housing benefit was established, not only did it face administrative problems, it also proved to be very costly both in administrative and benefit terms. The growth in benefit costs was largely attributable to government housing policies, involving pressure upon local authorities to increase rents. Since large proportions of local authority tenants were entitled to housing benefit the effects of these rent increases was to increase sharply the cost of the housing benefit scheme. When, in the mid-1980s, the Secretary of State for Health and Social Security came under pressure from the Treasury to make economies he found it convenient to make most of these in cuts in the value of the housing benefit scheme. The cuts were achieved by steepening the rate at which benefit tapered off as individual incomes rose. However, this taper-steepening intensified another problem – the problem of the 'poverty trap', the name given to the phenomenon by which individuals find that, as their earned incomes rise, they lose benefit income at rates above the highest income tax rates, because of reductions in means-tested benefits (see further discussion in Chapter 7). By the mid-1980s the combination of separate means-tested rules for different benefits, and in particular the difference between the rules used for family income supplement and the rules used for housing benefit, had the effect of making the poverty trap a serious problem. In some circumstances individuals might find that an increase of one pound in earned income led, after tax and benefit losses, to an actual reduction in income.

The recognition of the problem of the poverty trap made it urgent to establish a system in which the rules operating for the different systems of means-tested benefits were compatible with each other. The 1986 Act endeavoured to do this, although we will see, when we look at that policy in detail in later chapters, that the poverty trap problem has not been eliminated. However, in the changes which it made to the housing benefit scheme in the 1986 Act the government did eliminate some of the worst anomalies about the relationship between housing benefit and supplementary benefit. Just as rules relating to family credit were made compatible with those operating for income support, so too the rules relating to housing benefit were largely aligned so that most individuals with incomes at the level of income support entitlement could expect to get the same amount of housing benefit whether or not they were actually receiving income support payments.

Thus, we see that, at the centre of the reforms to social security associated with Norman Fowler (the 1986 Social Security Act) is the development of a structure with three benefits – income support, family credit and housing benefit – all based upon broadly similar principles. This is the development which was described earlier as edging the system slowly in the direction of negative income tax, and putting the operation of the means-tested benefit system very much at the centre of the overall design for social security. The fact that both family credit and housing benefit are expected to take income after tax and National Insurance deductions into account, rather than gross income as had been the case in the past, has been presented by the government as a move towards the idea of an integrated tax and benefit system. A much more detailed discussion of these measures in the next chapter will enable readers to decide for themselves the direction in which this set of social security changes is leading.

THE CHANGES BETWEEN 1979 AND 1989 – THE END OF THE BEVERIDGE SCHEME?

The 1960s and 1970s were described in the last chapter as a period when efforts were made to improve the Beveridge model of social security, but also as a period when the model was threatened by social changes and ad hoc additions to means testing. Can the 1980s, then, be described as a period when the Beveridge system was finally abandoned?

Certainly, the replacement of sickness and maternity benefit, for most claimants, by statutory sick and maternity pay took out a key part of the Beveridge structure. Unemployment benefit, on the other hand, remained comparatively unaltered. However, high levels of unemployment bringing large numbers of unemployment benefit claimants without National Insurance entitlements, either because they had exhausted them or had never qualified for them, did much to undermine this part of the Beveridge design. Flat-rate pensions remained substantially unaltered. However, all the insurance benefits suffered from changes to uprating rules which eroded their values and were further undermined by rises in housing costs, which, as we have seen, the Beveridge scheme never took into account. Finally, whilst it must be acknowledged that earnings-related additions were never a part of Beveridge's design, their coming did a great deal to protect the National Insurance scheme against some of its underlying weaknesses. In the 1980s earnings-related additions were abolished for short-term benefits, and their role in the pension scheme (SERPS) was reduced. At this stage it will be left to the reader to decide whether all this amounts to the end of the Beveridge scheme. It is a theme on which the next chapter will provide further evidence and to which subsequent chapters will return.

6. The Social Security System Today

INTRODUCTION

This chapter will describe the system of social security benefits in Britain in mid-1989. Where figures are quoted these will be for the benefit rates established in April 1989. Since benefits are uprated annually these figures will obviously soon become out-of-date, but where they are used they should convey to the reader some idea of their levels relative to each other.

CONTRIBUTORY BENEFITS

All employees, together with the self-employed, contribute on a weekly basis towards the National Insurance scheme of sickness and unemployment benefits, and pensions. They do so on an earnings-related basis, subject to a maximum contribution level. Normally these contributions are deducted by employers, who also have to pay additional contributions for their employees. These should not be confused with income tax deductions. There are different rates for those contracted in or out of the State Earnings-Related Pension Scheme (SERPS). The rules, operating from October 1989, are as follows. For employees not contracted out there is a lower earnings limit of £43 per week, below which there is no obligation to pay. People with earnings at or above £43 pay 2 per cent on the first £43 and 9 per cent on the rest of their earnings up to the upper earnings limit of £325 per week. Earnings above £325 are not assessed for contributions, which means that higher earners pay 9 per cent of £325 but no more. There are different rates (2 per cent less) for persons contracted out of the SERPS scheme. Rates for self-employed, and for non-employed persons who choose to be contributors, are different. It is not appropriate to go into this degree of detail here.

The National Insurance scheme provides a basic pension for all people who have been contributing for a significant part of their working life. For the contributor this is £43.60, with a basic pension for the wife of a male contributor (assuming she has not been a contributor herself) of £26.20. In practice most people retiring today will have their pensions either enhanced by the State Earnings-Related Pension Scheme (SERPS) or by a private pension. SERPS has been in operation since 1978 (although, for some, a more limited supplementary earnings-related pension scheme had operated between 1960 and 1975), with contributions gradually accumulating additional pension rights (it will take 20 years for full entitlements to be accumulated under SERPS). Assuming it has not been altered by the government – the 1986 Social Security Act reduced rights under the SERPS scheme! – full entitlement will be determined by a formula which provides a pension based upon 20 per cent of earnings.* This is complicated, since it does not mean that any individual will get 20 per cent of what they were earning before retirement, rather that it will be related, with adjustment for inflation, to earnings over the whole of their working life. Furthermore, this arrangement will be phased in gradually so that the first group to get the full entitlement will be people retiring in 1998 with 20 years of earnings since the inception of the scheme in 1978. After 1998 the reckonable period for earnings will extend, taking into account the fact that the system will have earning records for over 20 years. Clearly, records will not be available on the whole of working lives until somewhere beyond 40 years of operation of the scheme. Meanwhile broken employment records, as a result of unemployment for example, will reduce benefits, but special adjustments are made to mitigate the effects of broken employment as a result of 'home responsibilities' (looking after children or disabled persons).

The employee who is unable to work on account of sickness is initially dependent, since the enactment of the Social Security and Housing Benefit Act of 1982, upon his or her employer for support. The latter is, with some exceptions, required to provide sick pay, at least up to minimum levels prescribed by Parliament,

* There will be a brief period around the end of this century when more than 20 per cent will be paid (as high as 25 per cent in 2000). This complication arises because the 1986 Act modified a more generous earnings rule and the change is being phased in gradually.

for 28 weeks. The minimum statutory sick pay level is £52.50 per week for persons earning over £84 and £36.25 for persons earning between £43 and £83.99. Below £43 there is no entitlement, but it should be noted that persons earning below that figure do not have to pay National Insurance contributions. There are no 'dependants' additions' for recipients of statutory sick pay. After statutory sick pay, anyone still unfit for work moves on to National Insurance invalidity benefit, set at a flat-rate level. Assuming some National Insurance contributions in the past, this means (without going into complexities) in practice attachment to the labour force during at least half of the last two years; this will be a contributory benefit paid at £43.60 per week, with additions for a non-earning wife of £26.20 per week, and £8.95 for each child. There is also a state sick benefit scheme, providing benefits lower than invalidity benefits (standard rate £33.20 per week) for people in the first 28 weeks of sickness who have recent National Insurance contribution records but were not in employment immediately before they became sick. Also, those whose incapacity for work arises out of an industrial accident or a prescribed industrial disease may get special, higher, benefits after 15 weeks' incapacity for work. The level of benefit in this case depends upon an assessment of 'level of disablement' (ranging from an addition of £7.12 per week to the basic benefit for an adult at the bottom end up to £71.20 per week at the top).

There is a system of statutory maternity pay, similar to the statutory sick pay scheme (but with different pay rates), payable for 18 weeks, backed up by a reduced state maternity allowance available to women with recent work records who do not qualify for pay from their employers.

National Insurance unemployment benefit is available after three days out of work, subject to complex previous contributions conditions, like those for sickness and invalidity benefit but excluding the formerly self-employed. This is paid at the rate of £34.70 per week, for someone with the appropriate contributions record, with the possibility of additions of £21.40 per week for a wife but no additions for a child. After a year on this benefit entitlement is 'exhausted', and recipients cannot requalify until they complete a period of 13 weeks in work.

There are, for both sickness and unemployment benefit, rules designed to prevent abuse of the scheme. The rules with regard to unemployment benefits are, however, much more obtrusive. Claimants need to be able to prove that they are available for work. There are provisions for disqualification from receiving benefit for up to 26 weeks if individuals are judged to have left work voluntarily, lost their jobs through their own fault or refused a suitable vacancy. There are also rules to prevent persons involved in industrial disputes and seasonal workers from securing help from the unemployment benefit scheme. At the time of writing, the government is strengthening the various disqualification rules, requiring claimants to prove (as was the case in the 1930s) that they are actively seeking work.

Widows have an entitlement, based on their husband's contributions, to widowed mother's allowance, if they have children to support, and widows pensions if they are over 45. The rates for these are £43.60 per week, with additions for child dependants of £8.95 per week. There is also a lump sum payment of £1,000 available on widowhood, to widows under 60, or whose husbands were not in receipt of retirement pensions. Otherwise widows 'inherit' pensions, with a basic rate of £43.60 but with the possibility of SERPS additions. Widows lose their benefits if they remarry before the state retirement age; there is also a 'cohabitation rule' which may be operated to treat widows living 'as wives' in the same way as 'married wives'.

These, then, are the insurance benefits surviving from the Beveridge era. It should be noted that the basic assumptions about male contributions, and about wife's benefits being based upon husband's contributions, still survive. Wives may earn pensions and other benefits in their own rights, and some of the complicated rules relating to these situations have been left out of this discussion. Basically, wives and widows cannot simultaneously receive benefits 'earned' themselves and benefits 'earned' by husbands.

Since a later section will compare the benefit rates cited here with the rates for the means-tested benefits, to show how recipients of basic insurance benefits are likely to need supplementation from means-tested benefits, it is important to note that there will be many insurance benefit recipients who will have private benefits to support them when out of work. Many recipients of statutory sick pay will benefit from employment-related schemes which may be more than the statutory amounts, and many recipients of basic insurance pensions, including widows pensions, will also be in receipt of private pensions. The long-term sick and the unemployed, by contrast, are much more likely to be dependent on the basic benefits.

NON-CONTRIBUTORY, NON-MEANS-TESTED, CONTINGENT BENEFITS

Child benefit is paid, at a rate of £7.25 per child, to the parents or guardians of all children under 16, and children between 16 and 18 who are still at school. The only qualifying condition is one of residence. This benefit has not been uprated alongside the other benefits and tax thresholds in 1989 and the Thatcher government has made it clear that they are happy to see the value of this benefit eroded. Single parents may also obtain a modest additional benefit of £5.20, but only for the first child.

There are a number of benefits for the disabled, which are neither contributory nor means-tested. Severe disablement allowance is available for persons over 16 who have been incapable of work for 28 consecutive weeks. If they first became incapable before they were 20, there is no further condition for receiving this benefit. If not, they must be at least 80 per cent disabled (although this medical test is waived in certain circumstances – for the blind or partially sighted, for example). The current rate of severe disablement allowance is £26.20, with additions of £15.65 for an adult dependant and £8.95 for each child dependant. It should be noted that these rates yield, where no other income is available, incomes inferior to those provided by income support. Hence, they will normally need to be supplemented by the latter, so that for many people in the group it is the means test rates which actually determine income level, and application for this benefit may be regarded as irrelevant. Sixty per cent of severe disablement allowance recipients are women. The benefit was introduced to replace 'non-contributory invalidity pension' and 'housewives non-contributory invalidity pension'. The latter was accompanied by a controversial 'household duties test' which fell foul of a European Court ruling on civil rights. The new benefit opens up some increased opportunities for claims from severely disabled married women, but the 80 per cent disability test limits the scope quite stringently, and the payment is, as we have seen, very modest.

Attendance allowance, a benefit introduced in 1971, provides an allowance payable to those aged 2 or over who are so severely disabled that they need either frequent attention or continual supervision. There are two rates of attendance allowance, a higher one where day and night attendance is required of £34.90 per week, and a lower one where only either day or night attendance needs can be established, of £23.30 per week. These statements simplify a rather complicated set of rules, with interpretation resting upon medical judgements likely to be variable and open to challenge.

Mobility allowance, introduced in 1976, is a payment of £24.60 per week. It is payable to people with a physical disablement such that they are 'unable or virtually unable to walk or where the exertion required to walk would cause serious medical harm'. Claimants must be over 5, and the qualifying condition must be satisfied before age 65 and a claim made before 66. Claimants can only keep mobility allowance until they are 80, but no recipients will cease to qualify on age grounds before November 1994.

Invalid care allowance, also introduced in 1976, is a benefit payable to someone providing regular and substantial care, for 35 hours per week or more, to someone receiving attendance allowance. The current rate of invalid care allowance is £26.20 per week with £15.65 per week for an adult dependant and £8.95 per week for each child dependant. Like severe disablement allowance, and unlike attendance and mobility allowances, it is treated as a resource for purposes of calculating income support (see next section). Hence, again, its similar low rates mean that anyone receiving it who has no other income will also need to claim income support. Again, it has become available to married women (since 1986) but they must be able to show that they are full-time carers.

MEANS-TESTED BENEFITS

The central means-tested benefit is 'income support', which replaced supplementary benefit (itself the successor to National Assistance). People in full-time work (defined as working 24 hours or more) cannot apply for income support. Otherwise it is the principal means-tested income maintenance support benefit available to adults (see below some discussion of the special limits to help for young people) whose income (from whatever source) and capital are below government-defined levels.

Calculation of entitlement to income support involves a series of rules dealing with:

1. determination of personal allowances;
2. addition of premiums to those allowances where appropriate;
3. addition of some kinds of housing costs (although most are now dealt with in the separate housing benefit scheme);
4. subtraction of any income (with the amount to be taken into account modified by 'disregards' in some cases); and
5. the application of some rules relating to the treatment of capital.

The unit of assessment for these calculations is the claimant, the claimant's wife or husband (unmarried sexual partners of the opposite sex being treated as married spouses), and any dependant children. The next five paragraphs explain these rules in rather more detail.

The personal allowances taken into account in financial year 1989–90 are as follows:

- Single person or lone parent under 18   £20.80 per week
- Single person 18–24   £27.40 per week
- Single person 25 or over and lone parent 18 or over   £34.90 per week
- Couple both aged under 18   £41.60 per week
- Couple (at least one aged over 18)   £58.40 per week
- Dependent child (rates vary from £11.75 per week to £27.40 per week according to the age of the child)

The following are the most commonly added premiums:

- Family   £ 6.50 per week
- Single parent   £ 3.90 per week
- Single pensioner under 80   £11.20 per week

- Pensioner couple both under 80   £17.05 per week
- Disabled person or pensioner over 80   £13.70 per week
- Couple, one of whom is disabled or
  over 80   £19.50 per week

There are also special premiums for disabled children, and for the severely disabled (subject to a very restrictive test which excludes most people). The lower disability premium, on the other hand, is paid to any claimant who has been incapable of work over six months or where claimant or partner are in receipt of any long-term incapacity allowance, such as invalidity benefit or severe disablement allowance. In most cases, only one premium is paid (whichever is highest if more than one is applicable). Exceptions to this rule are that family premiums are paid to all families regardless of entitlement to other premiums, and that the disabled child and severe disability premiums are paid on top of other premiums.

When claimants are owner-occupiers with mortgages, the relevant interest payments are taken into account in determining the amount of entitlement to income support. However, owner-occupiers under 60 are restricted to 50 per cent of their interest payments for the first 16 weeks of benefit entitlement. All other housing costs are met through housing benefit, except that, at the time of writing, hostel charges and private residential care charges may be met through special income support allowances. Changes are expected which will shortly shift responsibility for support for these charges either on to the housing benefit or on to the local authority social services department (see further discussion in Chapter 8).

Most income received is taken into account in full against income support entitlement. It must particularly be emphasized that insurance benefits, child benefit, severe disablement allowance and invalid care allowance are treated thus. Attendance and mobility allowances are not taken into account. However, £5 of a claimant's, or partner's, gross earnings are disregarded. This 'disregard' is extended to £15 for people who receive the disability premium, higher pensioners premium, lone parent premium, or have been unemployed for over two years. There are also small 'disregards' given against charitable payments to claimants.

Finally, the rules about capital are that where claimants,

together with their partners or dependants, have over £6,000 they are not entitled to income support at all. Where they have less than £3,000, capital is disregarded. People with capital between £3,000 and £6,000 have their benefit reduced by a formula which assumes a 'notional income' of £1 for each £250 of capital (or part thereof).

Alongside the income support scheme is a means-tested benefit available to low-paid, full-time workers. This is family credit, and it has replaced family income supplement. The calculation rules for this benefit are based upon those for income support, with some additional complexities which cannot be set out fully here. The maximum credit is payable where net earned income is approximately equal to, or below, the personal allowances available to a family on income support. Hence, the government aim is to ensure that most families, where there is a full-time breadwinner, are better off than comparable families on income support. Above income support level, family credit is withdrawn at the rate of 70 per cent: that is, for each £1 of income above that level, 70p of credit is lost.

A separate means-testing system, administered by local government but subsidized by central government, operates to provide assistance for low-income people's housing costs and local taxation – that is, community charge or poll tax in Scotland and in England and Wales after April 1990, or rates in Northern Ireland and in England and Wales before April 1990. This scheme has the generic name of housing benefit, and the only housing cost issues falling outside it are mortgage and mortgage interest payments, together with (at the time of writing) certain special residential care charges.

The housing benefit scheme has been designed to be compatible with the two other major means-tested benefits. The income support rules, with a few special exceptions (for example, the capital 'cut-off' is £8,000 not £6,000), are used in the calculation of benefit so that anyone at or below income support level gets the full housing benefit entitlement. Thus, an anomaly which occurred before, under which people on housing benefit but not on supplementary benefit could be worse off than people on both benefits, has been eliminated.

One controversial feature of the housing benefit scheme, which was introduced in 1988, is the provision that, however low their income, everyone should have to pay at least 20 per cent of their local taxation assessment. The government, in introducing this provision, claimed to be adjusting the income support rates to allow for average rates (or community charge) in that scheme. Occurring together with other changes this was a concession with little practical meaning for the typical benefit claimant.

Under the former supplementary benefit scheme there were provisions enabling single payments to be made to help people with exceptional expenditures – removal costs, furnishing, house repairs, and so on. An elaborate body of rules dealt with these entitlements. The 1986 Act swept away single payments, but set up, in its place, the Social Fund, to be administered by a specially trained group of DHSS officers. Under the Fund there are two types of grant available as of right to people on income support or family credit: a lump sum maternity needs payment of £85, and a funeral needs payment (the amount of which depends upon funeral costs). There is also a provision for grants to be made from the Social Fund to assist with the promotion of 'community care'. These may be available when someone needs help in establishing themselves in the community after a period of institutional care, to assist with some travelling expenses to visit relatives in hospital and other institutions, and to improve the living conditions of defined 'vulnerable groups' in the community. Elaborate guidance is provided to Social Fund officers to help them determine needs of this kind: they are expected to liaise closely about such matters with social services and health services staff, and to take into account powers these other departments may have to provide assistance in cash or kind. Apart from the grants outlined in the points above, all other help from the Social Fund is by way of loans, normally repayable by weekly deductions from benefits. Again, officers have been given elaborate instructions on the circumstances in which they may provide loans.

The Social Fund, excluding the two items of benefit as of right, is 'cash-limited'. This means that local offices have annual budgets, and their staff are expected to relate a set of non-statutory rules about priorities to the total sum available. Indeed, they even have monthly spending targets to help them keep within the budget. The experience of the first year of the scheme was that there was a strong tendency to undershoot the targets, particularly on grants. In the second year, however, after a fast start, the system seems to be becoming self-regulating to ensure full expenditure of the budget spread smoothly over the year. Claimants for help from the Social Fund, other than claimants for maternity and funeral payments, have no formal right of appeal against decisions, although there is a provision for internal 'review'.

This description of the new structure for the main means-tested benefits does not exhaust the list of benefits. One quite important means-tested benefit administered by local authorities – entitlement to free school meals – had its availability restricted under the 1986 social security changes. Free school meals are now only available to children whose parents are on income support.

Other means-tested benefits include grants to students in higher education, relief from payment of National Health Service charges, and legal aid. Local authority social services departments also use means tests to determine charges for residential care and domiciliary services. It is not appropriate to go into these in detail here, but we will come back to some of the issues about compatibility between the principal state means tests and some of these specific means tests in Chapter 8.

INSURANCE BENEFITS AND MEANS-TESTED BENEFITS

At the end of the last chapter the question was posed, is the Beveridge scheme now defunct in Britain? Some general considerations were outlined which might help to answer that question. However, in practical terms, what is crucial in answering such a question is data on the number of situations in which individuals' incomes are actually determined not so much by the insurance benefit levels as by the means-tested benefit levels. Table 6.1 attempts to answer this question from official statistics, by comparing numbers on various insurance benefits with the numbers receiving income support supplements to those benefits. What it does not show, however, is the numbers who do not receive income support, but do still get means-tested housing benefit to supplement their income.

These figures seem to offer grounds for comparative complacency about the relationship between National Insurance and income support levels. However, if we examine this issue in

Table 6.1   Numbers on various insurance benefits and numbers
             with income support supplements to those benefits,
             1988–89

	(a) Numbers in receipt of the relevant insurance benefits (thousands)	(b) Number of those recipients in receipt of various supplements (thousands)	Col. (b) as % of col. (a)
Retirement pension	9,755	1,405	14%
Unemployment benefit	620	120	6%
Invalidity benefit	1,395	105	7%

Source: HMSO, The Government's Expenditure Plans 1989–90,
          Cm. 615, January 1989, ch. 15, p. 13.

another way we will find more disquieting evidence. The examples
below compare the basic National Insurance rates operative in
1989–90 with income support rates. These clarify the way the
systems work and bring in the issues about housing benefit.

● *Example A*. Healthy pensioner couple, both under 80, with
  only a basic insurance pension plus dependent wife's addition. Insurance pension £43.60 + £26.20 for wife = £69.80.
  Income support entitlement £58.40 + pensioner couple
  premium of £11.20 = £69.60. Whilst they would apparently
  have no entitlement to income support, being 20p over the
  limit, if one became disabled they would have an entitlement. Obligation to pay the community charge will give
  them an entitlement to the means-tested community charge
  benefit, and any housing costs will give them an entitlement
  to either housing benefit or (if owner-occupiers) to income
  support.
● *Example B*. Long-term sick man with a wife and two
  children aged 12 and 14. Invalidity benefit entitlement
  £43.60 + £26.20 for wife + £8.95 × 2 for the children =
  £87.70. Child benefit of £7.25 × 2 = £14.50 in payment.

Income support entitlement £58.40 + £34.70 for the two children + £6.50 family premium + £19.50 disability premium = £119.10 minus child benefit of £14.50 = £104.60. There is clear entitlement to income support in this example, as entitlement exceeds invalidity benefit by £16.90.

- *Example C.* Single unemployed man aged 24. Unemployment benefit £34.70 per week. Income support rate £27.40 (no premiums payable). Clearly it will be housing cost level which will determine whether this person needs to apply for a means-tested benefit. However, note that when he reaches 25 his income support rate goes above the unemployment benefit rate to £34.90. Even more importantly, if he remains unemployed for a year his insurance benefit will exhaust. It is important to note that, whilst Table 6.1 shows 740,000 people on unemployment benefit, the official table from which this statistic was derived showed 1,320,000 unemployed people dependent on income support without any insurance benefit at all.

- *Example D.* Unemployed man with a wife and two children aged 12 and 14. Unemployment benefit entitlement £34.70 per week + £21.40 for a wife (no child additions) = £56.10. Child benefit £7.25 × 2 = £14.50. Income support entitlement £58.40 + £34.70 for the 2 children + family premium of £6.50 = £99.60 minus child benefit = £78.60. There is an entitlement to Income Support, because this scheme includes child additions while the unemployment benefit scheme does not. However, this family is much worse off than the family in Example B.

Of course, many other examples could be used. The general points being made here are that:

1. income support and basic National Insurance levels are very close so that, whether or not income support is claimed, the income support level is in many respects more clearly the determinant of income levels than insurance; and
2. most households will, in any case, be within the qualifying scope for housing benefit, and, once the community charge has been introduced, many non-householders will similarly be in need of means-tested benefits to be able to pay that.

Beveridge's general defence of comparatively low insurance levels – although he would not necessarily have defended the ones we have got – was that incentives should remain for individuals to supplement them by private means. It is, of course, the case that many insurance benefit recipients do not need to supplement them with means-tested benefits because they have private pensions and savings and so on. However, the severity of the treatment of these by means tests must lead many people to ask whether it has been worth their while to accumulate small amounts of savings or to pay into modest pension schemes. On the other hand some insurance benefit contributors may well also wonder whether they should not perhaps have sought to evade the extra tax of the weekly contribution when it has brought so little or no extra benefit. This will, of course, depend upon the extent to which they are happy to be claimants of the means-tested benefits – an issue to which we will return in the next chapter.

THE COST OF SOCIAL SECURITY

In Chapter 5 it was stressed that the high cost of social security has been an important reason for changes in social security policy, and in Chapter 4 it was suggested that this was the rock on which many proposals to extend the Beveridge principle foundered in the 1960s and 1970s. It is appropriate, therefore, to end this account of the present-day system with some data on its costs.

The most up-to-date source on public expenditure is the government's annual account of past public expenditure and future plans. At the time of writing the last published source of this is a document published early in 1989, which shows that the estimated outturn for public social security expenditure in Great Britain for the financial year 1988–89 was £47,588 million. This represented 31 per cent of all public expenditure. While it was pointed out earlier that social security contributions are not today regarded strictly as an 'earmarked' social security tax, it is worth noting here that approximately £29,000 million was raised in this way. About half of this was from employees, and half from employers. This total, as will be seen from Table 6.2, exceeds National Insurance expenditure.

Table 6.2 shows the distribution of social security payments

Table 6.2 *Estimated distribution of social security expenditure between various benefits in Great Britain, 1988–89 (£ million)*

	Amount	Percentage of Total	Recipients of major benefits (thousands)
Retirement pension	19,390	41	9,735
Invalidity benefit	3,410	7	1,040
Unemployment benefit	1,143	2	755
Widow's benefit	908	2	395
All other insurance benefits	749	2	—
Total insurance benefits	25,600	54	—
Income support	7,650	16	4,925
Family credit	422	1	470
Housing benefit	3,817	8	4,465
Social Fund	164	0	—
Total means-tested benefits	12,053	25	—
Child benefit	4,522	10	12,015
Attendance allowance and invalid care allowance	1,202	3	770
Mobility allowance	655	1	540
Other 'contingent' benefits	1,132	2	—
Total 'contingent' benefits	7,521	16	—
Administration and miscellaneous services	2,414	5	—
Total	47,588	—	—

Source: HMSO, *The Government's Expenditure Plan 1989–90*,
    Cm. 615, January 1989, ch. 15, pp. 1–2.2.

between various benefits. We see how the cost of retirement pensions dominates, and, bearing in mind the issue about the balance between insurance and means tests in the system as a whole, it is important to remember how much the insurance side is dominated by pensions. Without that element, the total for insurance benefits would be £6,210 million – only half of the total of £12,053 million for means-tested benefits.

7. Issues about Social Security Administration and Benefit Delivery

ADMINISTRATIVE ARRANGEMENTS

The Department of Social Security is responsible for the social security system, and its remit crosses national boundaries in mainland Britain. In other words, the Department is responsible for social security in Wales and Scotland. There is a separate system in Northern Ireland, but in most respects it works with the same legal structure as that in mainland Britain.

Inevitably, a department which has to deal with large numbers of individual claims for benefit needs a network of local offices. These local offices are organized in a system in which there are regional offices and, in headquarters, a regional directorate which is responsible for the management of the whole devolved system. There are then other headquarters 'divisions' (subdivided into 'branches') with responsibility for policy matters. At the time of writing, the government is exploring the case for hiving off routine administration to quasi-autonomous organizations. Inevitably, the social security system is being considered as a possible case for this treatment.

In the last chapter we saw that social security benefits could be separated into three categories: insurance benefits, non-means-tested contingent benefits and means-tested benefits. Inevitably, rather different administrative issues apply to each of these groups.

Entitlement to an insurance benefit depends upon an individual's contribution record and, to keep track of these contributions, a national system has had to be devised. Therefore, if an individual makes an application for an insurance benefit through a local office, that office has to check against the large and

81

elaborate national contribution record system, at a central office in Newcastle upon Tyne, to determine entitlement.

A rather similar situation applies with regard to the most significant of the contingent benefits, child benefit. Here again there is a central office, based in the north-east of England, at Washington in County Durham, to maintain the child benefit records. In this case the whole administration of the system is run from Washington, and local offices are merely postboxes for enquiries.

The contingent benefits for the disabled, by contrast, are only paid after quite complex enquiries into individual circumstances. Therefore, their administration is very similar to that employed for the means-tested benefits: that is, decision-taking is based within the local offices. However, even in respect of the means-tested benefits, the shift towards an impersonal set of rules for determining entitlement is facilitating the centralization of administrative activities. In due course, there will be a shift away from local administration, with local offices becoming places where decentralized enquiry clerks meet the public and pass messages on to central computerized organizations, with VDU screens available to provide detailed information about individual cases. Such a development could leave only those benefits which require very detailed enquiries and discretionary decisions at the local level, such as the Social Fund, in the hands of local offices.

There are, however, two parts of the social security system which, while still in the control of the Department of Social Security so far as policy issues are concerned, are decentralized in rather different ways. One of these is the system of benefits for the unemployed. In this case, unemployed people who claim insurance benefits make their claims through unemployment benefit offices maintained by the Department of Employment. If, in addition, these individuals need to apply for income support, their applications are passed across from the benefit offices to the local social security offices. The latter will be responsible for the authorization of payments of income support which are then normally made through the unemployment benefit office. In this sense the Department of Employment are agents for the Department of Social Security in respect of benefits for the unemployed. This system, which is, in many respects, a legacy of the very early days of social insurance, is maintained to enable control to be exercised over claims for unemployment benefit. There are close connections, in this system, between the payment of benefits and the system of job advice and placement services for the unemployed. In the 1970s efforts were made to separate these two systems, it being argued that employment services should be separated out from the services directly concerned with the benefits for the unemployed. In the late 1980s that perspective has been turned on its head: a recent document (Department of Employment 1988) stresses the need to run the employment services and the system of benefits in a very close alliance. In this instance the Secretary of State for Employment has turned the clock back to the system characteristic of the 1930s, in which the central task of the employment service was to police the system of unemployment benefits.

A rather different form of decentralization applies in the case of housing benefit. Here, it is the local authorities which are responsible for the assessment and payment of benefit. The responsible local authorities are the lower-tier ones in England and Wales (districts and boroughs). In Scotland it is a little more complicated as, whilst the lower-tier local authorities are the housing authorities, the upper-tier authorities (the regions) are responsible for community charge collection and may accordingly adminster rebates of this. These authorities assess claims for housing benefit, and for community charge benefit, and are reimbursed by the Department of Social Security for almost all the cost. This reimbursement system is under review, in connection with changes in the system of support for local authority housing, and it is possible that the rate of reimbursement will fall in future. In certain special cases, local authorities may take decisions about marginal enhancements of individual benefits or about the treatment of high rents on which a lower rate of subsidy (25 per cent), or in some cases no subsidy, goes to them. The system of housing benefit is regulated by the Department of Social Security which provides detailed regulations for the local authorities and may audit and check local decision-making. Nevertheless, there is a range of issues about housing benefit on which officials have some degree of discretion at the local level, or at least some need to make difficult judgements about the facts of individual cases.

Finally, it should be noted that statutory sick pay and maternity pay involves, in a sense, decentralization of administration to employers.

DISCRETION

The subject of discretion, and in particular discretion in social security, has been a topic given substantial academic scrutiny in Britain. There has been a debate about the meaning of the concept (Bull 1980; Donnison 1982; Adler and Asquith 1981; Hill and Bramley 1986: ch. 9). In this presentation, the concept will be used very loosely (as it was in Chapter 4), treating as aspects of discretion decisions ranging from ones that are comparatively unfettered to ones which are the subject of elaborate regulation. In other words, the concept is applied both to rules which say little more than that officials may, in exceptional circumstances, enhance benefit to decisions where what is being required is a judgement, based upon very full regulations about, for example, degree of disability or whether or not an individual's claim to be a tenant of a dwelling is established.

The central concern of most academic analyses of the concept of discretion in social security has been the discretionary powers residing in the law and regulations relating to principal means-tested benefits – that is, in the system of income support or its predecessors, the systems of supplementary benefit and National Assistance. The system evolved, between its establishment in 1934 and the 1986 Social Security Act, in a way which can be broadly presented as a movement away from discretion. The transition from National Assistance to supplementary benefit in 1966 involved a much fuller Act of Parliament which enshrined rights to benefits comparatively clearly. However, the 1966 Act left open several important areas of discretion. Two areas which received much attention were a) the power to add weekly additions to benefits to meet recurring needs, and b) the power to make single payments to meet exceptional needs. But, in addition to these two issues, there were many other important discretionary issues. Two others which received some attention were the 'wage stop', a power existing under National Assistance and eventually abolished under supplementary benefit in 1975, which enabled officers to pay less than the full benefit where the consequence would be a benefit level above prevailing wage levels. The other was what used to be called the 'cohabitation rule', a rule necessitated by the absence of an individual means test so that a couple living together as man and wife could be treated as if they were married. Whilst the terminology has now changed, and the system deals with this issue in a more sophisticated way, this is an issue which has survived from the days of National Assistance to the present day. It is now an issue for both the income support scheme and the housing benefit scheme, and could well become of increasing importance under the rules relating to community charge benefit, since couples (including non-married couples) may be liable for each other's payments and once again, therefore, the benefit rules apply the means test to both *together*. These examples by no means exhaust the areas of discretion within the scheme; some others will be discussed more fully below.

However, first it is important to say more about the complicated history of discretion in respect of additions to benefits and single payments.

Chapter 4 described how, until the enactment of the 1980 Social Security Act, the law relating to discretionary additions and single payments did little more than give the Supplementary Benefits Commission the power to make additions. What then happened was that the Commission, and before it the National Assistance Board, issued an elaborate internal set of instructions – the 'codes'. These instructions, ostensibly secret but in fact much leaked, included working rules to help officers determine whether or not they should make these discretionary payments.

The codes did not eliminate officer discretion; in practice they gave elaborate guidance to officers on how to identify situations in which they might use their discretionary powers. This meant that individual chances of getting discretionary payments might depend upon a) the extent to which they were aware of the possibility of such payments, and b) the willingness of officers to draw claimants' attention to their discretionary powers. This left the situation very open to discriminatory decision-making. Not surprisingly, the evidence from this period suggested that some categories of claimants were very much more likely to get this help than others. There was a tendency for officers to distinguish between the 'deserving' and 'undeserving' poor (see Hill 1969).

The whole system was open to criticism from the pressure groups because it was a discretionary system, regulated by secret rules, offering individuals not rights to help but the possibility of getting help if they were recognized as 'deserving' cases. In the 1960s and 1970s, as was shown in Chapter 4, there was a growth of both pressure group and local welfare rights activity, involving circulation of information about the discretionary powers and pressure upon supplementary benefits staff to use those powers, resulting in a steady growth in discretionary additions and single payments over this period. In 1969 471,000 claimants (17.5 per cent of total claimants) had 'exceptional circumstances additions'. By 1976 this had risen to 1,431,000 claimants (48.7 per cent). Similarly, in 1969 500,000 'exceptional needs payments' (single payments) were made; in 1976 this rose to 1,114,000 (DHSS 1978: 122). With this growth the issue of discretion became one of managerial concern as well as one of welfare rights. It began to seem, by the 1970s, that the discretionary system offered an open-ended commitment to claimants, and as claimants became better informed and welfare rights campaigns became more active it would be increasingly difficult to check the growth of expenditure. For this reason, the managerial and welfare rights arguments came together in making the case for the replacement of a system of 'secret rules' by a system of regulations, setting out individual rights to additions and single payments (DHSS 1978). From the managerial point of view this was seen as offering the opportunity to circumscribe discretion. The proposals which were brought forward in the 1980 Act to do this involved both the development of an elaborate structure of regulations and the elimination of certain kinds of single payments. In particular, the new regulations made clothing grants, which had become the most common form of single payments, generally unavailable, and a special regulation limited them to exceptional situations of family stress. Hence, the 1980 Act did not, in the terms we are using here, abolish discretion, what it did was replace the discretionary rule-making of the Supplementary Benefits Commission by a procedure under which regulations were issued by the Department of Health and Social Security, and accordingly the Supplementary Benefits Commission was abolished. Furthermore, it provided for a situation in which officers would have to have regard to statutory, and publicly available, rules in determining entitlement in an individual case. However, it still left them considerable scope for variation in the efforts they made to identify the special needs and the criteria they used to determine whether a response was appropriate (Howe 1985; Berthoud 1985; Cooper nd).

In the first year or so after the enactment of the 1980 Act single payments fell sharply. Then, claimants and their advisers began to learn the game and recognize which things they should ask for in order to get payments. In some areas take-up campaigns were mounted, publicizing the regulations. Whilst the latter were complicated, and could not regularly be circulated amongst claimants, it became possible for advisers to identify the issues to raise. In practice, therefore, people began to learn that they would have to meet clothing needs out of the basic grant, but that there was a wide range of circumstances in which they could ask for grants for furniture replacements and so on. The managerial aim to curb single payments had not been achieved, and the expenditure growth trajectory went on upwards. Single payments rose from just over a million in 1981–82 to 4 million in 1984–85 and 5½ million in 1985–86. At this stage the cost of single payments had reached over £300 million per year, and the government took steps (as a preliminary to more radical changes planned for the 1986 Act) to limit payments by altering the regulations on eligibility.

Hence, the Department of Health and Social Security, not to be so easily defeated by the welfare rights movement, and under great pressure from the Treasury to cut public expenditure, decided to have another go at the problem. Its response was the 1986 Act which effectively abolished additions and rights to single payments. The system of premiums developed for the income support system was designed to replace the structure of additions by standard elements in the grants going to claimants. Hence premiums were introduced for the elderly, with enhancements for the older elderly, disabled people and single-parent families, designed in part to take account of the tendency of these groups to get additions to the standard benefit under the old scheme. So far as single payments were concerned, with the exception of the special provisions of maternity grants and funeral grants, the system has in practice turned back to discretion; and these two provisions constitute the sole entitlement to single payments within the Income Support scheme. The Social Fund, which replaces the old system, permits no rights to benefits; instead a

Social Fund manual gives guidance to social security officers on the exercise of their powers under the Fund. By contrast with the 'codes' of the past the manual is a public document, although so far as the positive aspects of discretion are concerned it does not identify rights to payments. Government has solved the managerial problem in quite a different way and by two means. One is to cash limit the Social Fund budget, thereby forcing officers to give attention, when making decisions, to budgetary limits and accordingly requiring them to see cases in a relationship of priority to each other. Second, a significant part of the Social Fund budget is only for loans rather than grants. The budget for 1989–90 is £203 million, but 70 per cent of this is for loans and only 30 per cent for grants. Thus, the actual cost of the scheme will be lower because loans, by definition, will be repaid.

Grants are described as community care grants, with an emphasis on their provision to assist individuals moving out of institutional care into the community. There *are* powers for grants to be given to help people to be maintained within the community, but the manual places these generally as of lower priority and requires officers to be very reluctant to give them. Not surprisingly, given the cash limited budget, the first year of the Social Fund scheme was characterized by substantial underspending of the grants budget with wide differences between local offices. However, at the time of writing, it looks as if the budget will be fully spent in most local offices in the second year. Loans are not merely limited by the fact that there are elaborate instructions in the manual on circumstances in which officers may or may not give loans, but also by the fact that, although interest-free, they are repayable out of individual benefits. Because there are strict rules about the amount of an individual's benefit that may be deducted for loan repayment in this way, there are situations in which individuals are refused loans on the grounds either that they are already overcommitted by the repayment of existing loans or that they have other kinds of debt commitments which would make it impossible for them to repay loans. Hence, whilst we see in the Social Fund a very distinct return to discretion, this phenomenon is very different to that which operated in the 1970s. Cash limiting and the loan concept provide a means for the Department of Social Security to control rigidly the impact the welfare rights movement can have upon this area of social security expenditure. As has already been suggested, the issues about discretion in social security are not confined to the widely discussed problems of additions and single payments. An idea of the wider character of the issue can be obtained by examining the areas where official judgements may be required in one particular scheme. Whilst new income support rules severely circumscribe the scope for discretion within that system, many of the other issues about discretion are still very relevant to the administration of housing benefit. Looking at the housing benefit scheme, one can detect discretionary issues in connection with the three key parts of the decision-making framework: the determination of income and capital; the determination of the nature of the household; and the nature of the rent commitment. Let us look at each of these in a little more detail.

So far as income is concerned, the position with regard to individuals on benefit income is fairly straightforward; the complications arise where there is earned income. For this, decisions may need to be made about the evidence produced about earned income, and about the way in which variable income is taken into account. There are particular difficulties posed by housing benefit applications from individuals who are self-employed. The kinds of self-employed people who make applications for housing benefit are, not surprisingly, those whose businesses are, to say the least, 'marginal'. Some of these people may actually be making losses and drawing upon capital; many of them lack professional accountants to help them keep a record of their affairs; and some of them are in a good position to procure income which is not revealed either to tax or social security authorities. It will be seen, therefore, that housing benefit officers may have a number of quite complicated investigatory and decision-making problems to deal with in connection with applications from this group of people. There may be similar problems about the rules relating to the determination of capital resources under the scheme, where for example the capital is held in a foreign country or in property or, of course, where the individual makes efforts to evade the disclosure of capital. There is a special set of rules in the housing benefit regulations to deal with situations in which individuals may be deemed to have deliberately reduced capital by what the authorities regard as extravagant expenditure, in order to qualify for benefit; they give authorities discretion to 'assume' the continuing availability of spent capital.

Turning now to the question of the problems associated with determining the nature of the household, reference has already been made at the beginning of this section to the long-standing issue of 'cohabitation'. Since couples living together as man and wife are treated differently, under means-testing rules, from people living independently there may be controversial decisions on this point. But, in addition, in a multi-occupied household there may also be room for doubt as to who actually is the tenant, and exactly what the rent-paying obligations are within the household. The system has a series of complex rules about householders and about contributions from non-householders, with allowance made for the possibility that there are joint householders. The interpretation of these rules, or more particularly the application of the rules to specific situations, may all raise issues which require discretionary judgements (Loveland 1988).

Finally, the issue of determination of the appropriate rent level for rebating purposes may also raise problems. There are some quite elaborate rules to determine situations in which it would be unreasonable for a public authority to be expected to meet the rent in full. The rent may be unreasonably high or the accommodation unreasonably opulent and spacious for the claimant. In dealing with high rent the local authorities are put under further pressure to exercise their discretion by the fact that they may not get full subsidy for support of high rents. This depends on a judgement on these issues made by a Rent Officer. This is a complex issue about the relationship between social security policy and housing policy, an issue to which we will return in the next chapter.

In addition to specific discretionary issues with regard to the determination of basic entitlement to housing benefit there are two other significant discretionary clauses in the housing benefit regulations, both of which relate to additional discretion given to the local authority. One of these is a regulation which enables housing benefit to be enhanced in exceptional circumstances, broadly, that is, where there are special reasons for regarding the existing rules as operating unfairly for a specific individual. Such payments are strictly limited in aggregate amount and do not attract Department of Social Security subsidy. The other is a power to enable the local authority to backdate a claim for benefit for up to a year. This only attracts a 25 per cent subsidy. It is worth noting that discretion in relation to backdating crops up in all sorts of places in our social security structure, although within the main social security benefit system there is some quite elaborate case law regulating its use (see Ogus and Barendt 1988: ch. 15).

The issue of case law raises one further point about housing benefit to which it is important to draw attention. Although the housing benefit system is regulated by the Department of Social Security there has been no systematic attempt to make the legal structure for housing benefit identical to that for income support. In the case of issues about all the benefits directly provided by the Department of Social Security, except for the Social Fund and some other minor and very obscure issues, there is provision for the dissatisfied claimant to appeal to a Social Security Appeal Tribunal. There is also provision for an appeal from a tribunal to a national quasi-judicial official, the Social Security Commissioner, on a point of law. So we have a situation in which, in addition to the Acts and the regulations, there is a body of social security case law to which reference can be made. There is no comparable provision for housing benefit. Instead, the only recourse available to the aggrieved housing benefit claimant is an appeal to a locally constituted Housing Benefit Review Board. The members of the Review Board are the elected members of the local authority responsible for that housing benefit scheme and there is no recourse to further appeal; although of course the actions of Review Boards have to be in conformity with the general tenets of administrative law, so that in the event of exceptional disregard of the law individuals may take matters to the High Courts. Each Review Board is therefore a 'law unto itself'. There is no requirement for Review Board decisions to be compatible with each other, or with those from other local authority areas, and no provision to ensure that housing benefit decisions are compatible with quasi-legal decisions taken under the social security appeal system.

Finally, it would be wrong to complete this section on discretion without drawing attention to three other areas where discretionary powers may be quite important. One of these is in the area of the law relating to unemployment benefit. Individuals who claim unemployment benefit may be refused benefit on the grounds that they have lost jobs through their own fault (for example, they have left of their own accord or been sacked for some form of misbehaviour at work), if they have refused suitable offers of employment, or if they are not actively seeking work. Interpretation of these rules requires some quite complex judgements on the part of unemployment benefit office staff. In relation to this area of discretion, elaborate case law has built up over the years, through appeals to the Social Security Commissioners (see Ogus and Barendt 1988: ch. 3). Nevertheless, cases can be complex and discretion still has to be exercised.

The second area of discretion relates to disability benefits. Here we move into a different kind of discretion – that exercised by medical experts in making judgements about levels of disability and capacities for self-care activity. Here we find again a complex body of case law and also a wide range of issues where judgement is essential. Evidence on wide differences in success in obtaining mobility allowance or attendance allowance suggests discretion is a significant phenomenon in this area of policy.

Third, the statutory sick pay scheme gives employers a responsibility, shared before its introduction by the social security authorities and the medical profession, to 'police' claims for support from individuals whose status as 'sick' may be open to question. This is an area of discretion which has so far remained uninvestigated.

THE TAKE-UP OF BENEFITS

Social security benefits are paid on receipt of an application from an individual. In many cases there is also a requirement for regular reapplications for benefits. A situation of this kind inevitably produces variations in the extent of 'take-up' by specific individuals.

We may contrast two opposite views about the issue of take-up. On the one side there is the view that individuals have rights to state benefits, and that it should be the duty of the state to ensure that individuals are fully informed about those rights and obtain all to which they are entitled. The exponents of this view therefore expect the social security system to be an open one, which publicizes its services very fully and which is ready to help individuals to identify all the things to which they are entitled. In the absence of this it is also regarded as entirely appropriate that there should be services, run by pressure groups or voluntary agencies or even run by government agencies, which assist people to identify rights to benefits and secure their full entitlements.

The alternative to the rights perspective is a view that benefits which are too easily available will be open to abuse. It is believed that individuals will turn to state benefits in situations in which they could make provision for themselves, and that they will be inclined to defraud benefit systems. When this perspective is put into practice, situations will be found in which individuals find it difficult to get information about benefits and find that the benefit application process is complicated. Whilst this second perspective is rarely openly expounded by official spokespersons, there seems little doubt that a widespread view of this kind has contributed to making the system obscure and difficult (Golding and Middleton 1982).

This book is being written at a time when it is difficult to give accurate estimates on take-up levels, because of the introduction of a new system of benefits. In the mid-1980s the take-up of supplementary benefit was estimated (DSS 1987) by the Department of Social Security to be about 76 per cent of possible claimants. The take-up of family income supplement was estimated to be 54 per cent. The housing benefit take-up was estimated, in the same report, to be 90 per cent for 'certificated claimants' (people in receipt of supplementary benefit) and 58 per cent for 'standard' (other) claimants. The same report pointed out that take-up was partly related to level of entitlement: in other words, much non-take-up was amongst people with comparatively small levels of entitlement. Hence take-up as a percentage of the total possible expenditure was estimated at 89 per cent for supplementary benefit, 76 per cent for standard housing benefit, 94 per cent for certificated housing benefit and 65 per cent for family income supplement.

The introduction of the new system, in 1988, is known to have had an, at least initially, adverse impact on take-up. Family credit take-up has been much lower than the government expected – indeed so seriously low that the government has engaged in an expensive advertising campaign. Housing benefit take-up will probably also have been adversely affected by the end of the 'certification' procedure for income support claimants.

We may identify a hierarchy of state benefits with, at one end, benefits for which the take-up is close to 100 per cent and, at the other end, benefits whose take-up is quite low. At the top end of this hierarchy are benefits which are particularly simple in character, with a simple test of entitlement. Child benefit stands out as an example of this since the claimant has to do no more than prove that she (or, sometimes, he) is responsible for the care of a child and is resident in the United Kingdom. It is also true to say that most of the insurance benefits have high take-up rates. Individuals are aware of their entitlement to a pension, and can be expected, on retiring, to make an application. Similar considerations apply to sickness and invalidity benefit. The situation with regard to unemployment is a little less straightforward, because here we find a number of barriers to claiming which have been set up to prevent abuse of this benefit.

So we see the insurance benefits at the top end of our hierarchy, and we also see with them the contingent benefit of child benefit. Sadly, we do not find that the contingent benefits for the disabled have similarly high take-up rates. In the case of mobility allowance and attendance allowance the problem seems to be the complexity of the rules relating to entitlement to benefit. However, with this reservation, we nevertheless may generalize that the insurance and contingent benefits tend to have higher take-up rates than the means-tested benefits.

It is, however, within the group of means-tested benefits that we find very great variations in the levels of take-up. It is generally believed that the means-tested benefit with the highest take-up is one which will not be considered in this book, the means-tested grant available to university students. It has been suggested that the high take-up rate here is associated with the coincidence of both a straightforward personal circumstance – that is, admission to university – together with the fact that the individual is in a situation in which no issues of stigma apply. Setting that benefit on one side, we may then look at the main categories of means-tested benefits. The take-up for income support is likely to be higher than for the other benefits (as the data given for supplementary benefit above suggests), which must be attributable to its centrality in the meeting of individual need. People with no other source of income at all will inevitably turn to this benefit, as will individuals with very low levels of income from the insurance system. The take-up of income support is likely to rise with the amount to which the individual is entitled. The position with regard to housing benefit is that individuals who are entitled to income support are likely to be advised of, or recognize, their entitlement to housing benefit as well, wherever they are householders. The main problem of take-up in relation to housing benefit occurs therefore amongst the group of people who are not on income support. Here low take-up is likely amongst individuals with earnings. In the years before the introduction of housing benefit it was shown that council tenants, at that stage entitled to rent rebates, were very much more likely to be claimants than private tenants entitled to rent allowances. It also seemed to be the case that individuals, generally owner-occupiers, who were only entitled to rate rebates were likely to be low claimants. Now these benefits are all embraced within the housing benefit scheme, but it is likely that the differential claimant rates will still apply. We may at this stage speculate that the new benefit, to be attached to the housing benefit scheme, to provide rebates from the full payment of the community charge will similarly tend to have a low level of take-up. Individuals who qualify for this, who did not previously qualify for housing benefit, are unlikely to be aware of a potential entitlement. This group of people will also be significantly a young and mobile group, whose circumstances and income change frequently, and who may be very unsure about their levels of entitlement. In many authorities the administration of this benefit, at least for non-householders, will often be the responsibility of a Finance department, with no other rebate responsibilities and a preoccupation with tax collecting.

Family income supplement, introduced in the early 1970s, always had a comparatively low take-up. As a benefit going to the earning poor, its qualification conditions were particularly obscure and individuals were unlikely to be aware of their entitlement. In replacing family income supplement by family credit in 1988 the government argued that the new simpler benefit, with its qualifying rules more comparable to those for income support and housing benefit, would be more likely to be taken up than family income supplement. As has already been said, early evidence suggests that that is not correct.

These, then, are the principal facts about the issue of take-up. Let us now turn to the various factors which will have an impact upon this issue. These comprise a variety of things, some of which interact with each other. There is the issue of problems about lack of knowledge about benefit. Closely related to this is the problem of the complexity of benefit systems. These two phenomena may also contribute to, and be reinforced by, the administrative complexity associated with the benefit system; individuals may find that it is particularly difficult to get benefit, and that they have to encounter a great deal of administrative hassle. The next issue that we may identify is one which has been widely debated, in the context of take-up of social security benefits – the issue of stigma. Associated with stigma is the fact that individuals expect, or fear, negative consequences to flow from making claims for specific benefits. Finally, there is an issue about low take-up in situations in which individuals expect that there will be a lack of significant gains from claiming the benefit. In discussing the last of these issues we will move on to two specific problems about means tests in social security: the 'poverty trap' and the 'unemployment trap'.

Factors Affecting Take-up

Knowledge of benefits

Reference has already been made to the issues about knowledge of benefits. There are manifestly significant differences in the extent to which individual benefit systems are publicized. It may be generally observed that, by contrast with the enormous government effort put into, for example, the selling of the nationalized industries, comparatively little effort is put into advertising the availability of state benefits. Over the years the government has provided a range of leaflets distributed through such places as post offices and libraries, but there is little wider advertising of benefits on television or on posters for example. It may be added, however, that the recent family credit take-up campaign, mentioned earlier, is a significant exception to this generalization.

There is manifestly a dual problem for individuals here of a) identifying that they belong to a category for whom benefit is available, and b) of recognizing the availability of that benefit. The problem of knowledge is further complicated by divisions within the system. We have seen, for example, that housing benefit is administered by the local authorities and not by the Department of Social Security. Therefore, the many individuals who qualify both for benefits directly administered by the Department of Social Security and for housing benefit have to apply to separate offices which may be sited in very different places. Even within the central government-administered group of benefits there are divisions; unemployment benefit and income support for the unemployed depends upon a claim through a Department of Employment unemployment benefit office, and even the benefits directly administered by the Department of Social Security may involve different parts of different offices for insurance benefits and means-tested benefits.

Complexity

One cannot really analyse the problem of lack of knowledge separately from the issue of complexity. So far as complexity is concerned we may identify a variety of problems. First, the peculiar history of social insurance has meant that individuals have become quite confused about the relationship between the paying of contributions and the claiming of benefits. To many people the apparently rather essential distinction between the insurance benefits and the means-tested benefits is by no means a clear one. This is particularly the case in relation to the benefits for the unemployed. In this case, for many individuals, the first introduction to the system, as young workers without insurance records, is to the process of claiming for income support. Only subsequently do such individuals learn, after a period in work, about the insurance benefit systems. Not surprisingly, they find it difficult to draw a clear distinction between the two, and that difficulty is compounded by the situations in which they need to claim both. It may similarly be suggested that the use, throughout the social security system, of rules about 'claimant units', rooted in the old idea of the dependence of women upon men as well as the dependence of children upon their parents, sows confusion about entitlement, particularly for women. There may also be some problems where the woman is the 'manager' of the household budget but the man is normally required to be the benefit claimant.

However, the central issues about complexity obviously relate to the elaborate rules concerning the means-tested benefits. In order to claim income support, family credit, or housing benefit individuals have to fill in long and elaborate forms. It is difficult for them to anticipate in advance what they will receive, and of course it is particularly difficult to cope with the complexities of the 'tapers'. The issues about the tapers are naturally particularly significant for individuals amongst the earning poor, who would be likely to be entitled to family credit and housing benefit, but obtain less than the full amount because of their earning levels. Whilst reference has been made above to the large government advertising campaign on family credit, being carried out at the time of writing, it must be added that this, probably necessarily, involves very simplistic statements about levels of benefit likely to be achieved. It certainly does not mention one very real 'catch' for claimants: that if they are already getting housing benefit then payment of family credit will substantially reduce the level of that benefit!

The problem of administrative hassle

Once again, what is to be said in this section links back significantly to what was discussed in the last section. Reference has already been made to the complicated forms that individuals have to complete in order to get benefit. Those forms require them to fill in details about family circumstances, about sources of income, and, in the case of housing benefit, about the rent and tenure of their accommodation. Alongside the information supplied on forms, individuals are likely to have to provide evidence to back up the statements they make – to have to produce rent cards or to provide wage slips for example. In the past many applications for means-tested benefits were made by way of personal visits to local offices at which clerks carried out interviews and filled in forms. Now it is perhaps more common for individuals to have to fill in the forms themselves and submit them to a local office for scrutiny. However, they may then find that they have to be interviewed by officials who require them to substantiate aspects of their claims. They may also find that they may need to visit an office to find out what is happening to their claims.

We may compare and contrast the two approaches to claiming. Both entail difficulties and, sometimes, hassle. Where a personal claim is made, individuals have to submit to a lengthy interview in which their personal circumstances are revealed to another individual. That individual may be hostile to them, or may at least be suspicious about the statements they make. The ambience of the office in which the claim is made may, in various respects, be degrading, so that individuals find attendance there a disturbing process. On the other hand, the formal application by way of the completion of an elaborate form also has a deterrent aspect. Having to fill in a form, containing a series of questions which may not apply very precisely to individual circumstances is often a difficult process; and is clearly more difficult for people with comparatively low levels of literacy or whose first language is not English. A multi-paged form which asks a great deal, not merely about individual circumstances but also about other members of the family and household, may be difficult to complete. There are clearly, therefore, pros and cons of the two methods of making an application for benefit. Unfortunately, there are many circumstances in which individuals experience the disadvantages of both. They visit local offices where they have a long wait, and are perhaps put off by the attitudes of officials or by the atmosphere or by the characteristics of their fellow claimants, only to emerge at the end of the process with a difficult form to take home and fill in. They complete the form and send it in, and then find that nothing happens and that they have to call again at the office to try to get a result.

Administrative hassle extends, of course, beyond the initial claim for benefit. The initial payment of benefit may be delayed or there may be an error when the money eventually arrives. On receiving the benefit the individual is reminded of an obligation to report all changes of circumstances. Therefore a variety of subsequent difficulties may emerge over time. This is particularly significant where individual circumstances are changing regularly as will be the case with many individuals with earnings. Thus, people with rapidly changing circumstances may find the system particularly deterrent. Finally, in the interests of the prevention of fraud it must be noted that claimants of benefits receive, in written and sometimes also in verbal forms, severe warnings about the consequence of false statements. These may be worrying to claimants who are unsure about their rights, and have difficulty in stating the facts of their cases with great precision.

Stigma

In describing the various kinds of administrative hassle that claimants may experience, some references have already been made to characteristics of the system which may stigmatize claimants to benefit. In the past, the very strict controls surrounding the administration of the Poor Law made application for means-tested benefits a very degrading process, and it has therefore been argued that the stigma of the Poor Law extends today to the means-tested benefits which are its successor (see discussion in Deacon and Bradshaw 1983). On the other hand, it has also been argued that the shadow of the Poor Law extends only over the older generation, who are therefore much more conscious of the stigma of claiming means-tested benefits, and that fewer and fewer claimants today share those memories. However, the very existence of a distinction within our social security system between those benefits to which people have contributed (the insurance benefits) and the benefits which are non-contributory and means-tested surely tends to keep the concept of stigma alive within the system. This distinction reflects, and in some cases amplifies, stigmatizing distinctions within our society. As Marsden put the issue with regard to unsupported mothers 'our society defends the institution of marriage by stigmatising them' (Marsden 1973). A similar point may be made about the propagation of the value of work by stigmatizing the unemployed. In some respects, moreover, in an affluent and materialistic society to be poor, for whatever reason, is to feel stigmatized. With such a feeling one will be reluctant to draw attention to one's plight.

From time to time governments have made efforts to attack the problem of stigma. This was particularly evident at the time when National Assistance was replaced by supplementary benefit in 1966, when the government went to some lengths to stress rights to benefits, particularly for pensioners. Early in the 1970s when the Supplementary Benefits Commission, under the leadership of David Donnison, played a particularly active role in the politics of social security, we saw a range of efforts to encourage individuals to recognize that they had rights to means-tested benefits.

Nevertheless, efforts to stimulate a view that individuals have rights have, sometimes simultaneously, been counteracted by campaigns to increase the vetting of social security claims (see Golding and Middleton 1982). The widespread publicity given to cases where individuals have been convicted of defrauding the social security system, political campaigns which have emphasized the number of fraudulent claims, and measures adopted to try to identify individuals who could be working but are claiming benefit have all contributed to keeping the problem of stigma alive (Deacon 1978; Golding and Middleton 1982).

As suggested in the previous section, an individual's experience when he or she makes a claim for benefit may influence the extent to which he or she feels stigmatized. Obviously the behaviour of front-line staff in social security offices will be important in this respect. So too will conditions in the offices: their state of cleanliness, the nature of the furniture and the waiting times have an influence upon the sense of stigma. In many cases it does not help that offices have grilles to prevent the public getting easy access to staff and that furniture is screwed to the floor to prevent it being thrown around. These latter points remind us that the feeling of stigma stems not only from the behaviour of officials in the system but also from the associations felt when making a claim for benefit. A feeling, however inappropriate, that whilst one is a legitimate claimant one is standing in a queue, or sharing an office, with other people who seem to be illegitimate claimants must have some impact upon an individual's attitude to being a claimant. Stevenson has described this as 'stigma by association' (Stevenson 1973: 21). It is an inescapable fact that social security offices are likely to contain many highly deprived, desperate and demoralized people. The minority of claimants who have severe social problems, and are most distrusted by social security clerks, are likely to be particularly evident amongst visitors to a local office because they will have to work particularly hard to progress their claims. To be more explicit, local offices are likely to have a lingering quota of such groups as chronic alcoholics and individuals who have tramped from district to district and whose distrusted claims are being investigated at length. Such people will be misperceived by the casual visitor to a social security office as 'typical claimants'.

Negative consequences flowing from claims to benefits

As suggested above, manifestly negative consequences may flow
from claims which are in any sense fraudulent. In practice,
warnings against fraud will act as deterrents to individuals who
have nothing to hide. Individuals may fear consequences which
are not applicable. However, in some cases official efforts to
minimize claiming will lead to particularly strong emphasis upon
the potentiality of negative consequences. This is particularly
evident in the area of benefits for the unemployed. We have
already seen that, since its inception, the unemployment benefit
system has been hedged around with rules which involve the
reduction or elimination of benefits to individuals who have left
jobs, who have been sacked from jobs or who fail to take jobs
they are offered. In various respects the system also contrives to
remind claimants of the importance of continuous efforts to find
work. Regardless of the feasibility of getting work, unemployed
people are likely to fear that their lives will be under continual
scrutiny once they have claimed benefits.

The receipt of state benefits may expose individuals to fear of
other kinds of intrusion into their lives. Obviously an illegal
immigrant who claims benefit may run the risk of identification
and deportation, but there are also immigrants to Britain, whose
entry to the country has been conditional upon being non-
claimants to benefits, whose circumstances change rendering them
desperately in need of help. Beyond these two groups will be other
individuals with a perfect right to remain in Britain and to claim
benefits in Britain who nevertheless may feel, in a climate of
racism, that those rights will be challenged if they make themselves identifiable to the official benefit system. The behaviour of
officials, in some cases of this kind, have not helped with this
matter (Gordon and Newnham 1985). Immigrants, and black
claimants in general, are likely to find that questions about their
status in Britain are raised regardless of whether they are applicable to their cases, and that they are likely to have to prove their
rights in ways that do not apply to other people.

In general, becoming a benefit claimant involves getting your
name upon an official register which will draw attention to you,
and if you have anything to hide as a result of previous behaviour
you may feel that you are putting yourself at risk in this situation.

With the coming of the community charge a further consequence of being placed on any register monitored by the state is that this will make it easier for authorities to trace you for the payment of current, past or future taxes. A low-income person who, perhaps because of previous non-claiming, has fallen into arrears with community charge payments may find that making a claim for benefit leads to action for their recovery. In this sense the community charge, like the medieval poll tax, may contribute to the creation of 'outlaws' who fear the consequences of being identified by the state.

Whilst there may be circumstances in which individuals with severe financial problems, and debts, will find that becoming a benefit claimant enables them to secure some stay of action against them, it will nevertheless be the case that, if receiving benefits, they may be more liable to forms of direct collection of debts. Fuel boards and companies may make arrangements with the Department of Social Security to secure direct payment from benefits and, in some circumstances, so may public or private landlords. Also, it is relevant here to point out that the Department of Social Security itself is in a very strong position to secure repayment of debts from its own claimants. This, as we have already seen, is a central feature of the Social Fund, where the Department of Social Security is able to ensure that it gets direct repayment of the loans which it has itself made.

Lack of real gains

It may seem a little odd to include amongst the determinants of low take-up of benefits the fact that, in some circumstances, individuals may experience little gain from getting benefit. It may be argued that this can hardly be seen as a problem. Benefit systems will have rules about who qualifies and who does not qualify, and the fact that some people qualify for little or nothing is a natural consequence of these rules. However, this is a very important subject, and is one which needs to be put in the context of what has been said earlier about problems of knowledge and administrative hassle. It has been identified that individuals may often be unaware of entitlements. It has also been observed that low take-up is particularly significant where benefit levels are low.

A word of warning is appropriate about the use of the word

'low' here. What counts as a low gain in income for a low-income person is likely to be a very much smaller amount than would be the case with a high-income person. It is all very well to brush aside some of the concerns about low take-up by pointing out that many of the benefit losses are 'low', but these 'low' amounts may be vital to many people.

Nevertheless, applying for benefits tends to lead to a variety of situations of great uncertainty, and in which individuals may be put to great inconvenience, with an end result of only minimal gains. One experience such as this may then deter future claims, even if the gains could be quite considerable. But the whole problem is further intensified by two problems particularly associated with means-tested benefits and which have been identified as the 'poverty trap' and the 'unemployment trap'.

We shall deal with the unemployment trap first, since it is the simpler of the two phenomena. There is always a possibility with benefit systems that situations may arise in which it is disadvantageous for individuals to seek work, since their income may be less in work than it has been whilst on benefit. As was pointed out earlier in the chapter, until the 1970s the National Assistance/ supplementary benefit system had a provision known as the 'wage stop' to prevent it paying benefits above the wage levels individuals were likely to achieve. This was abolished at about the time that family income supplement was introduced. The coming of a benefit available to the working poor largely eliminated the phenomenon that the 'wage stop' was designed to prevent. However, it put in its place a situation in which individuals were likely to find that, on moving off benefit into work, they moved from a comparatively simple set of means-tested rules associated with supplementary benefit, to a more complicated set of rules associated with family income supplement and housing benefit. The actual experience of going into work may be, or may be believed to be (see Millar, Cooke and McLaughlin 1989), one of losing a secure weekly income from the state and putting in its place a low earned income, made still lower by the operation of emergency taxation, and a long wait for the new kinds of state benefits to which the individual is entitled. Obviously that situation will be even worse for those individuals who have imperfect knowledge of what they are entitled to at this transition point. It has been shown that individuals are deterred from taking low-paid work by these uncertainties, and government efforts have been made to try to prevent this deterrent effect. The introduction in 1988 of family credit to replace family income supplement was presented by the government as an important development to deal with the problem of the 'unemployment trap'. Family credit, it was argued, is a benefit that is easier to understand and therefore its application rates would be higher. It has already been pointed out that those application rates are not, at the time of writing, particularly high, and some of the government propaganda on the benefits to individuals starting work has been quite seriously misleading. There is still therefore some degree of uncertainty about the movement from unemployment into full-time work.

The situation with regard to part-time work is very much worse. Individuals in part-time work may still obtain income support, but as was shown earlier the levels of disregards for part-time earnings are low. What this means is that, once the individual has enjoyed the benefit of the disregard, any subsequent earnings will be offset pound for pound against their benefit up to the point where, of course, they lose benefit entirely. There are therefore strong deterrent effects against obtaining part-time earnings.

It may be objected that it is not appropriate to include this discussion of the 'unemployment trap' in a discussion on low take-up since it is, in a sense, an issue about 'unnecessary' take-up. Inasmuch as the unemployment trap operates, it involves people being deterred from taking work. However, it is also, as has been shown above, in some cases an issue about low take-up of benefits available to people in work, arising because people do not recognize that they could gain by claiming them. There is obviously here a need to separate out the actual deterrent effects, evident enough in relation to rules relating to income from part-time work, from those effects which occur because people do not understand the system, as in the case of the underclaiming of family credit.

Moving now to the problem of the poverty trap we find here a more complicated phenomenon which has to be explained not in terms of the contrast between situations of 'in work' and 'out of work', but in terms of the impact upon individuals in work of small increases in earnings. Consider the example of a low-paid worker who is entitled to both family credit and housing benefit. What happens when that worker receives a pay rise of £1 per week?

First, that additional pound may be reduced by 25 pence income tax and by social security contributions which may be as much as nine pence in the pound. If these are taken into account, therefore, the actual gain from that pound increase in income will already have been reduced by 34 pence. Then, the remaining 66 pence affects the individual's entitlement to family credit which has a 70 per cent taper. That means that family credit will be reduced by 70 per cent of that 66 pence, leaving the individual with no more than a 20 pence gain. However, that is not the end of the story. Even this small residual gain will affect the individual's claim to housing benefit. The housing benefit taper, if the individual is entitled to both rent and community charge rebate, is 80 pence in the pound. Thus, that remaining 20 pence will be reduced by 80 per cent of it, giving an eventual net gain from that pound increase in gross income of only 4 pence. That is the stark reality of the poverty trap.

Before the 1986 Social Security Act the poverty trap effect was more haphazard and could amount to over 100 per cent, a bizarre result in which individuals could secure income increases but nevertheless end up worse off. The 1986 Act, in requiring the family credit and housing benefit systems both to work with net, rather than gross, income, and in requiring the family credit calculation to be operated before the housing benefit calculation, had the effect of reducing losses to below that 100 per cent threshold. But to the individual who experiences a 96 per cent poverty trap that is small consolation.

These poverty trap figures should obviously be contrasted with the tax effect for high earners, where the highest rate of income tax is now only 40 pence in the pound and National Insurance increases are capped by an upper earnings limit. It is therefore fair to say that the group of low earners, who fall within the range within which the poverty trap operates, face 'tax rates' markedly higher than the highest rates of tax.

This particular problem highlights issues particularly associated with the high family credit and housing benefit tapers. For many people only housing benefit or family credit will be paid, so that only one of these tapers will apply. Indeed, the interaction between housing benefit and family credit is such that, for many people, there is little point in claiming family credit because of its serious negative impact upon housing benefit entitlement. This raises some complex issues for both benefits and about the way their rules relate to each other. However, even for those individuals only on family credit the taper rate is 70 per cent, and for those only on housing benefit the rate is 80 per cent. With two benefits which taper off very steeply it must be recognized that there comes a point at which the individual loses entitlement to the benefits altogether. At that point, of course, the loss from the pound increase in income is then reduced solely to the losses entailed with the income tax and insurance contributions. There is an important policy question, therefore, about the range of incomes across which the poverty trap effect operates. Broadly speaking, the larger the family size and the higher the rent, the longer the individual will be in the poverty trap situation. In many cases, that can be a very wide income range indeed, so that even as much as a £50 increase in gross income will afford the individual comparatively little rise in net income. The phenomenon is illustrated in Figure 7.1, produced by the government, which plots gross weekly earnings against actual weekly spending power once tax and insurance payments and social security benefits are taken into account. Where the slope is gradual the rate of net spending gain is very slight.

It will be seen, therefore, that the poverty trap is an important problem for the operation of means-tested benefits for low-income workers. There are effectively two ways of designing a system which avoids it. One of these is to have universal family benefits and perhaps universal housing benefits which go to all families regardless of income. The second is to maintain means-tested benefits but to let them taper off very much more slowly. Both of these solutions are obviously costly. In the first case benefits go to large numbers of people who are also taxpayers. In the second case means-tested benefits extend a long way further up the income distribution.

So long as we have the poverty trap there are also choices as to how it should operate. It is possible to conceive of a system in which there would be a very sharp break somewhere along the income distribution after which there would be no entitlement to benefit. That would produce a very severe poverty trap indeed (well over 100 per cent) at a particular point in the income distribution, and it would therefore probably be associated with the unemployment trap phenomena discussed earlier. In other

Figure 7.1 Illustration of the poverty trap

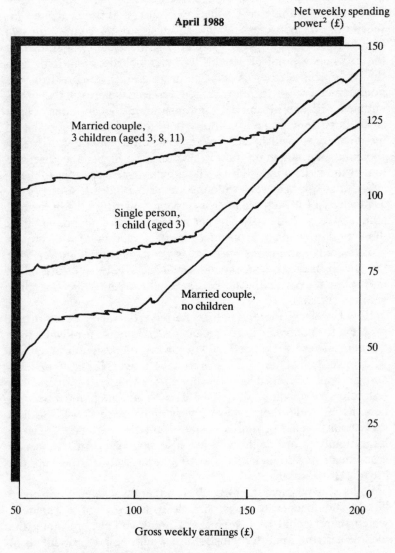

April 1988

Net weekly spending power[2] (£)

Married couple,
3 children (aged 3, 8, 11)

Single person,
1 child (aged 3)

Married couple,
no children

Gross weekly earnings (£)

2 Gross earnings from full-time work where
   head of household only is in employment

Source: Department of Health and Social Security
(Copied from *Social trends,* 19, 1989)

words there would be a very severe deterrent effect through increasing income at that point and it could give rise to a situation where there would be dependants on state benefits below that point and earners above it. The alternative is to spread the phenomena as widely as possible. The logical end point of this would be that means-tested benefits would extend a long way further up the distribution. In the absence of that, what we have is a comparatively steep taper, but nevertheless a taper which spreads quite a long way across the income distribution. In the final chapter of this book the issue of the poverty trap will again be brought into sharp focus when we look at alternative models for the social security system.

CONCLUSION

This lengthy chapter has dealt with many of the issues about the implementation of the benefit system. Chapter 8 will focus upon the implementation issues which derive their importance from the fact that the social security system operates alongside, and inter-relates with, other policy systems. Let us, however, summarize the issues covered so far. The chapter started with a general account of the way the social security system is administered. It then went on to outline the range of issues about official discretion in the system. That discussion was followed by consideration of a closely related issue – the incomplete take-up of the benefits – which was examined by detailing the various reasons for incomplete take-up.

Both the discussion of discretion and the discussion of take-up indicated that the problems with these phenomena, both for administrators and claimants, vary between benefits. This is an issue that needs some final consideration in general terms. Broadly it may be suggested that there is a hierarchy of benefits, with the insurance benefits and some of the contingent benefits involving few administrative problems, while at the other extreme there are complex means tests, as for housing benefit, and highly discretionary systems, in particular the Social Fund, for which the issues about discretion and take-up are very complex and their attendant problems for some claimants are very severe. Accordingly, the presence or absence of these problems is drawn upon in arguments for and against particular approaches to the provision of benefits. The simplicity of insurance and contingent benefits is seen as an argument for such systems by 'universalists' (see Townsend 1975: ch. 9). On the other hand simplicity can imply either high costs to the Exchequer or benefit levels which are low and poorly adjusted to individual needs (Titmuss 1971).

Probably the simplest benefit of all, with correspondingly high take-up and minimal scope for official discretion, is child benefit. To claim this, people have to do little more than show the presence in their household of a child for whom they are responsible. Implicitly, the insurance benefits seem to require claimants to show simply that they have been contributors. In introducing social insurance in 1909 Winston Churchill implied that he was replacing 'moralities' by 'mathematics'. In practice it is not as easy as this. Whilst for pensions, proof of age, and in some circumstances retirement, is all that is necessary, proving sickness can be more difficult and, so far as unemployment is concerned, qualification for benefit is hedged around by quite complex and controversial rules. The contingent benefits for disability are also subject to often complex rules, which make discretionary judgements by officials and doctors important, and may lower take-up.

Within the group of means-tested benefits there are also substantial differences. The structure adopted for income support eliminates many areas of official judgement and rule obscurity. In contrast, housing benefit was shown, in the discussion of discretion, to be still a very complicated system. Finally, of course, there is the Social Fund, which is at the extreme boundaries of the discretionary end of the spectrum.

These are considerations, then, for the evaluation of Britain's present benefit system. The evidence on issues like 'rights', the comprehensibility of benefit systems, the 'poverty trap' and so on also needs to be used in judging alternatives to the present system.

8. Interaction Between Social Security Policy and Other Public Policies

INTRODUCTION

Any comprehensive discussion of social security must give attention to the impact of the income maintenance system upon other areas of public policy, and vice versa. It is important to recognize that issues about social security are involved in two very important kinds of policy choices. One of these is the choice of whether to subsidize specific individuals; the other, closely related to this, is the choice of whether to provide benefits in kind or in cash. To explain this general point let us explore it in relation to an issue which will not be more fully explored in this chapter since, in practice, it has comparatively little impact upon the social security system because of the nature of the policy choices which have been already made. The issue is public transport policy.

Public transport may be subsidized for the general benefit of the population – to reduce the impacts consequent upon a free market, such as undersupplied services in some areas. But it may also be subsidized to enable low-income people, without private means of transport, to travel. If it is generally subsidized the subsidy will be a universal benefit – like child benefit – going to both rich and poor. The only impact of such a subsidy on social security will be that it may affect the levels of benefit given, since transport costs will not figure significantly in any cost of living calculation. However, an alternative approach to this issue may be to provide travel cost concessions for low-income people. Such people may, as is generally the case in Britain, simply be identified in broad categories – such as old people, children, students – in which case the implications for social security policy will again be minimal. But suppose, instead, a transport system decides to use a means test to determine entitlement to concessionary fares.

111

Then its decisions will start to interact with social security decisions. Anomalies will arise if its means test is either more or less generous than other means tests. Its means test will probably also contribute to the poverty trap. Its officials will want to check other benefits and perhaps be eager to work out an administrative liaison 'passport' scheme with other means tests to simplify decisions.

The latter scenario only describes one of the simpler options in this area; politicians often choose more complicated alternatives. It is possible to have a system whereby the transport enterprise is required to balance its books, but other public agencies may subsidize fares. In this case, the former will be interested in maximizing fares, knowing that the latter will protect poor people from their real impact, while the latter will see it as necessary to protect its scheme from abuse. Another alternative is a system where the transport enterprise will offer concessions to win customers but will want to ensure those concessions are not available to people who can obtain their fare subsidies from other sources. There are other possibilities.

With systems of special concessions for some customers of agencies generally subject to strict financial disciplines, whether market-imposed or not, a great deal of ingenuity tends to be devoted to trying to ensure that costs are carried by someone else. We will see, in specific sections below, how some of the issues outlined in general terms here have emerged and evolved in the relations between social security and housing policy and, in a variety of situations relating to local government charging policies in the personal social services and education (and to the related issue of private care services).

Whilst these types of issues are of great importance for the interactions between social security and the other public policies, we must not disregard some very different kinds of issues. One of these, also of great concern to local government, has been the issue about the extent to which the roles of public sector workers, concerned to provide services for low-income people, should embrace helping such people to deal with income maintenance problems. In Britain, at the centre stage in this respect, has been the relationship between social work and social security, where the concerns of social workers with the overall welfare of their clients have inevitably led them into concerns about the operation of the income maintenance system. It is no accident that the social problems which overwhelmingly come to the attention of social workers are those of the poor, often exacerbated by poverty.

The other interaction, discussed at the end of this chapter, is one already mentioned from time to time in this book – the interaction between social security policy and employment policy.

SOCIAL SECURITY AND HOUSING POLICY

When the government first developed subsidies to local authorities to build homes for low-income people, in the Housing Act of 1919, those subsidies were for the provision of properties and not for the direct subsidy of people. Initially, no attempt was made to force local authorities to adopt rent policies for these properties which took into account tenants' incomes. Local authorities were first permitted to adopt rebate schemes – varying rents according to income – by the 1930 Housing Act. This Act redirected the focus in local authority housing activity towards slum clearance, and there was some concern that many of the poor families in need of rehousing would be unable to afford the prevailing local authority rents. Thus rebates would concentrate the new slum clearance subsidies to the benefit of the poorest tenants. In practice, local authorities were slow to use these new powers. There was some political opposition to means testing, and general levels of Exchequer subsidies were in fact sufficiently high to enable the modest redevelopment programmes to proceed without rebates. Moreover, at that time, the spread of working-class incomes was so narrow that it was hard to devise rebate schemes which did not in practice apply to most tenants.

It was during the 1950s and 1960s that governments increasingly encouraged local authorities to adopt rent rebate schemes to concentrate the benefit from subsidies. First, advice was offered about the various types of rent pooling, rent setting and rebate policy that were considered good practice. The government gave several examples of rebate experiments and argued that they assisted a local authority to allocate accommodation to applicants in accordance with their true needs for houses of particular sizes and types.

The 1965 Housing Subsidies Act reduced Exchequer subsidies and relieved local authorities of the obligation to make contributions to their housing revenue accounts from the local rates. This was justified on the grounds that 'there is no doubt that the rents of a large number of council houses are at present being subsidised to a larger extent than the individuals require' (Hansard 1955). It was perceived as necessary to increase rents and support this through the introduction of various types of rebate scheme. A Ministry of Housing circular (29/56) gave local authorities various examples of available schemes but offered no firm statement about which should be chosen.

Nevertheless, the Conservative government increasingly turned to veiled threats as a means of encouraging higher rents combined with rebate schemes.

> In determining the amount of subsidy which the Exchequer should pay, the government are entitled to assume that councils will pursue reasonable rent policies and the changes now to be made in the subsidy arrangements will encourage them to do so. The assumed income for the purposes of the test (twice the 1956 gross value of all the houses in the authority's account) is based on the conviction that local authorities can, if they so wish, adopt rent policies which would assure them a total rent income of that order, while still enabling them to adjust to the needs of the tenants. (HMSO 1961)

White Papers in 1961 and 1963 stressed the need for 'realistic' rent policies and claimed:

> . . . hundreds of authorities have shown that rent rebate schemes can be worked fairly and without difficulty; and nothing is more unfair, whether to tax- or ratepayer, than that he should be compelled to subsidise the rent of a tenant who does not need it. (Ministry of Housing and Local Government 1963)

Similarly, in the later 1960s, when the Labour government was trying to get local authorities to limit rent increases, it commended 'differential rent schemes'.

This incremental development was extended to the whole system by the Housing Finance Act of 1972 which began a process aimed at securing a nationally determined system of 'fair rents' for all local authority tenants. This involved significant rent increases to be offset by rent rebates provided by local authorities on the basis of a scheme laid down, and partly subsidized, by central government. It also provided a similar system of rent allowances for private sector tenants, enabling local authorities to make payments in this case. These two schemes joined a national system for rate (local taxation) rebates which had been established in 1966.

The adoption of these national schemes highlighted the problem that the supplementary benefit system was also subsidizing the rents of many low-income people through its rent additions to benefit payments. Before 1972 arguments had already developed about whether or not tenants on supplementary benefit were eligible for rent rebates. Local authorities argued that they were not and that they should continue to receive the full unrebated rent from the Supplementary Benefits Commission; this greatly reduced the cost of their rebate schemes. On the other hand, the Supplementary Benefits Commission was equally keen to reduce its own costs and argued that supplementary benefit claimants should not be excluded from such schemes.

After the 1972 Act a very complex policy was initially developed with different rules for short- and long-term supplementary benefit claimants. The result was a muddle. Then in 1974 the system was changed to one whereby supplementary benefit met all net rents regardless of whether or not rebates or allowances were in payment, and local authorities were required to reimburse the Department of Health and Social Security where rebates or allowances could have been, but were not, in payment. This simplified the system administratively but left what became known as the 'better off' problem – that is, there were some people on rebates or allowances but not on supplementary benefit who would have qualified for the latter, and in consequence have received higher incomes, had they been paying full rents. There were also people on supplementary benefit who would have been better off with rebates or allowances and not on supplementary benefit at all. The whole issue was moreover further complicated by the fact that qualification for supplementary benefit could be a 'passport' to other means-tested benefits.

When the supplementary benefit scheme was reviewed in the late 1970s this problem was examined and it was suggested that the ideal way to resolve this problem would be for the rebate and allowance scheme (including the rate rebate scheme) to meet all housing costs. This idea was adopted in the 1982 Social Security and Housing Benefit Act. However, this was a rushed piece of legislation, motivated as much by a desire to cut administrative costs for central government as by a wholehearted commitment to rationalization (Hill 1984). It did indeed give local authorities responsibility for operating the new housing benefit scheme to meet the housing costs of all low-income people apart from owner-occupiers and some categories of lodgers; but in so doing it created two categories of beneficiaries, one of which included persons who received housing benefit automatically on proof of entitlement to benefits under the central means-testing scheme whilst the other included low-income people not benefiting from the national scheme who had to submit themselves to a locally administered means test. Problems about this dichotomy led to the need for further reform, which came about in the 1986 Social Security Act.

This legislation has, as shown earlier, largely transferred the support of housing costs to the local authority-run housing benefit scheme, eliminating most of the earlier anomalies. However, it is still appropriate to repeat the reservation of the Supplementary Benefit Review report, about this approach to rationalization:

> . . . any substantial changes to the existing arrangement could raise other problems, for example on coverage, entitlement, benefit levels and costs. Any form of integration would be likely to involve either an increase in costs which could not be accommodated within current expenditure plans without sacrificing other expenditure objectives or substantial problems of redistribution of current benefits. The familiar problem of the 'poverty trap' would also need to be taken into account. . . . And, to extend, beyond the limits of the current supplementary benefit scheme, the number of those who would look to public funds to meet up to 100 per cent of their housing costs, while advantageous to ill-housed families of low paid workers, would raise wider social and economic issues. (Department of Health and Social Security 1977: 58)

The government has opted to deal with this problem by adopting severe 'tapers' for housing benefits, discussed already in Chapter 7. In effect, it has controlled the cost problem at the expense of the poverty trap problem. Furthermore, any action the government takes to push up rent levels in general tends to increase the costs of the housing benefit scheme. In the early 1980s, therefore, we saw The Department of the Environment adjusting general subsidies to force local authority rent increases, and the Department of Health and Social Security responding to the 'knock-on' effect of this on housing benefit costs by steepening the tapers, complaining that the scheme was extending 'too far up the income distribution', a logical consequence of rent increases.

The local authorities and the benefit recipients are more or less passive recipients of the consequences of conflicting government policies. However, some local authorities, generally those under Labour control, have tried to influence this interaction by seeking ways of increasing rents which would be wholly or largely subsidized by central government whilst keeping other rents down. They have been frustrated in that search by the inevitable readiness of the Department of Health and Social Security to amend the housing benefit regulations to close such 'loopholes'. That, then, is a summary of how policy interaction has developed so far as the rents of local authority-owned houses are concerned. But housing benefit also covers private sector rents, and these involve other problems.

There would probably be a broad consensus of opinion that if you have a benefit scheme which takes into account the level of an individual's rent, and may, if income is low enough, meet that rent in full, rules are needed to prevent landlords taking advantage of the scheme by charging exorbitant rents to benefit recipients. However, that consensus crumbles, at least in Britain, when consideration is given to the right way to achieve this end. One way is to have a separate system of rent control, independent of the housing benefit scheme. That view is opposed by those – including the present Conservative government – who have been quite happy to see the system of rent control crumble in the face of evasion and creeping deregulation. This has led to the necessity for a control system, within the benefit scheme, to 'protect public funds' since, if benefit is available to pay any rent, market forces clearly do not provide any alternative control.

The method used to provide this control within the housing benefit system is an elaborate regulation to be enforced by the local authority. The key part of the regulation reads as follows:

(2) Subject to paragraphs (3) and (4), where the appropriate authority considers –

a) that a claimant occupies a dwelling larger than is reasonably required by him and others who also occupy that dwelling (including any non-dependants of his and any person paying rent

b)   to him) having regard in particular to suitable alternative
       accommodation occupied by households of the same size; or
       that the rates for the claimant's dwelling are unreasonably high
       by comparison with the rates payable in respect of suitable
       alternative accommodation available elsewhere;
       or
c)   that the rent payable for his dwelling is unreasonably high by
       comparison with the rent payable in respect of suitable alterna-
       tive accommodation elsewhere, the local authority may treat the
       claimant's eligible rates, or, as the case may be, eligible rent, as
       reduced by such amount as it considers appropriate having
       regard in particular to the cost of suitable accommodation
       elsewhere and the claimant's maximum housing benefit shall be
       calculated by reference to the eligible rates or eligible rent as so
       reduced. (Housing Benefit (General) Regulations 1987)

This rule is further qualified in paragraphs 3 and 4 by clauses
restraining its application where hardship would result from an
enforced move, and also requiring authorities to delay its operation where the rent had been met without the aid of benefit in the
past. It would not be appropriate to go into these qualifications in
great detail here; what is important is that they leave a considerable amount to the discretion of the local authority.

In the past, I have run a considerable number of short courses
designed to train local politicians in how to operate the Housing
Benefit Review Board system for which they are responsible. The
interpretation of the regulations related to high rent is always a
central preoccupation of these events, and where authorities have
made restrictions they have, not surprisingly, attracted appeals. It
is interesting to note the ideological dilemmas the regulations pose
for people at both ends of the political spectrum. Conservatives
worry about the conflict between their interest in supporting
private landlords and their concern for public expenditure
restraint. Labour members tend to want to curb 'profiteering'
landlords, but are concerned about the impact of restrictions upon
the welfare of tenants. Labour-controlled local authorities have
probably been less zealous implementers of rent restriction than
have been Conservative ones (Loveland 1987, 1988). The tightening of regulations indicates that the government has been concerned about the under use of restriction.

However, the whole issue of rent restriction within the housing
benefit scheme has been brought into sharper focus by the

government's efforts to deregulate the private housing market. There are already many loopholes in the rent regulation system, but now the government intends that many tendencies should be what will be termed 'assured tenancies' with 'rents freely negotiated between landlord and tenant'. Nevertheless, the White Paper proposing the legislative change enacted in the 1988 Housing Act, had this to say about the role of housing benefit:

> The housing benefit system will continue to provide help to those who need it. However, once rents are deregulated it will be necessary to ensure that landlords cannot increase the rents of benefit recipients to unreasonable levels at the expense of the taxpayer. Local authorities' discretion to restrict benefit on unreasonable rents is already being strengthened as part of the housing benefit changes to take effect in April 1988. The Government proposes in addition to require Rent Officers to scrutinise the level of rents which are being met by housing benefit. Where a rent is excessive, the subsidy to the local authority will be restricted to an appropriate market rent for the dwelling in question. Guidance to Rent Officers on the principles for assessing rent levels will be issued by the Secretary of State. The Government is prepared if necessary to place direct limits on housing benefit, rather than on subsidy. (HMSO 1987: para 3.18)

There are three points in that quotation which require further discussion. First, local authorities are directly reimbursed by the Department of Social Security for most of their housing benefit expenditure. Hence, they have little incentive to implement quasi-discretionary regulations they dislike. There is no doubt that some authorities – particularly in the London area where accommodation demand exceeds supply, rents have risen sharply, and many landlords have already found ways to evade rent controls – have rarely applied the housing benefit rent restriction rules. Quite apart from any ideological considerations, the fact that they would have to deal with any homelessness caused by the application of these rules has been a deterrent. Consequently, the government has applied a penalty to such local authorities in the form of a restriction of subsidy. Authorities will only get 25 per cent subsidy for any amounts paid in excess of limits determined, case by case, by Rent Officers.

Second, in the last sentence of the quotation, we see the government making a further threat – in case subsidy restriction does not work – to intervene directly to limit benefit levels.

Third, the government obviously needed some local agents if they were to impose either of these measures. It could have developed a system of local rent ceilings: this was done temporarily but, recognizing the rigidity of this approach, the government then gave the task of determining housing benefit rent limits to a group of public officials, independent of local authorities and accountable to central government, namely Rent Officers. As the Housing Act had taken many of their earlier rent fixing powers away, these officials were in need of a new task if they were not to become largely redundant. However, the Rent Officers only determine, bearing in mind the rules quoted on p. 117–18, appropriate rent levels to attract normal subsidy. Local authorities still have to decide whether – despite the fact they will only get a 25 per cent subsidy for any 'excess' expenditure – they should use their discretion to give further help. In practice this means that the local authorities must consider the following regulation dealing with the issues of the availability of suitable alternative accommodation and the feasibility of a move.

(6)   For the purposes of this regulation –

a)   in deciding what is suitable accommodation, the appropriate authority shall take account of the nature of the alternative accommodation and the facilities provided having regard to the age and state of health of all persons to whom paragraph (7) applies and, in particular, where a claimant's present dwelling is occupied with security of tenure, accommodation shall not be treated as suitable alternative accommodation unless that accommodation will be occupied on terms which will afford security of tenure reasonably equivalent to that presently enjoyed by the claimant;
       and

b)   the relevant factors in paragraph (3) are the effects of a move to alternative accommodation on –

(i)   the claimant's prospects of retaining his present employment;
       and

(ii) the education of any child or young person referred to in paragraph (3) (c) if such a move were to result in a change of school. (*Housing Benefit (General) Regulations* 1987)

If there is any dispute about these powers the 'appeal' situation is most complicated, and, in my view, most unsatisfactory. A local authority may 'appeal' against a Rent Officer's decision, but that decision will then be reviewed by a senior Rent Officer. A claimant may 'appeal' to a Housing Benefit Review Board, consisting of local councillors, for the authority to use its discretionary powers to pay above the rent limit. There is no opportunity for the claimant to try to prove to the Rent Officer system that the rent limit chosen was wrong.

The logic of the government's position on 'assured tenancies' and housing benefit is that it wants a free market to operate but has the problem that, for some tenants, the payment of benefit (hypothetically up to any rent level) means that they will not behave as a free 'bargainer' normally would. However, in Britain, private renting is already a very bad deal, compared with buying, for most free agents in the marketplace. Hence, a high proportion of private renters are low-income people who rent because they lack the resources to buy. They are, therefore, the very people most likely to be applicants for housing benefit. Hypothetically the 'assured tenancies' proposal could lead to an unexpected revival of the private market with very different kinds of tenants moving into it. But the economic relationship between renting and buying makes that most improbable (Kemp 1988). If Rent Officers prove to be zealous restricters of rent and, as seems very likely, local authorities are unwilling to bear the cost of overriding such decisions, and if the supply of housing to low-income people in the areas of housing pressure does not increase, many people are likely to remain in accommodation only partly subsidized through the benefit scheme, drawing on their other resources to bridge the gap between their officially allowed rent and the actual rent they have to pay. We will have partial rent restriction by way of the housing benefit scheme, with many poor people paying premiums where excess demand prevents that from working satisfactorily.

We see, then, a complex relationship between some aspects of social security policy and some aspects of the working of the housing market, with a new government policy for the latter being accompanied by the elaboration of the former. The ways powers are exercised within the housing benefit system – by central government in the elaboration of the regulations restricting rents and the controls over local decisions, by the local authorities in interpreting the regulations, or by Rent Officers who are supposedly autonomous but could well become explicitly accountable to central government for their performance of their new task – will be very important for the future working of the private rented housing market and for the welfare of low-income people 'trapped' within it.

This section has also repeated, and amplified, some past history because the evolution of the various problems about means-tested housing support provides a very good illustration of the kinds of problems which arise with differential pricing systems based upon means. Some similar cases will be mentioned in the next two sections but will not be so fully discussed.

SOCIAL SECURITY, LOCAL AUTHORITY CHARGING POLICIES AND COMMUNITY CARE

In Britain, after the enactment of the 1948 National Assistance Act, it became taken for granted that income maintenance was a central, rather than a local, function.

However, since 1948 local government has continued to play a role in the British income maintenance system by providing a variety of special grants and benefits in kind – educational grants, school meals, various forms of domiciliary and residential care, subsidized transport and so on, together with subsidized housing as discussed in the last section. Broadly, these local contributions to income maintenance have taken two forms:

1. relatively indiscriminate subsidies to all users of the services (which may imply some explicit targeting of help to the more needy but may be quite indiscriminate and perhaps biased towards the better off, as with education, free libraries and subsidies to the arts); and
2. means-tested benefits or services designed to subsidize or reduce the burden of costs for low-income people.

Traditionally the contributions of the Poor Law to income maintenance were distinguished as 'indoor' and 'outdoor' relief. The modern equivalents to this distinction are the provision of 'institutional' and 'community' care. The Poor Law reform of 1834 had sought to limit relief to the able-bodied poor by imposing the 'workhouse test', requiring them to enter repressive institutions in order to secure support. Outdoor relief might still be extended to those unable to work. The evolution of the system over the next 100 years reversed this distinction to some extent. Forms of institutional care were developed for the old and sick, and many of the rudimentary hospital services for the poor were developed within the Poor Law. On the other hand, it became recognized as desirable, particularly in the face of unrest in the 1920s and 1930s (see Gilbert 1970) over unemployment and the inadequate coverage of the contributory benefits for this relief, to extend means-tested outdoor relief to the able-bodied unemployed. Hence the reforms of the 1940s centralized 'outdoor relief' and transferred the Poor Law hospitals to the newly established National Health Service. Institutions providing care which did not involve substantial medical services remained the responsibility of the local authorities.

The new division of responsibility, although it removed income maintenance from the local level, did not free local authorities from concerns with their clients' incomes. They now had to determine whether those given residential care were able to contribute towards the costs of that care, and to work out arrangements with the National Assistance Board to settle who should carry the burden of these costs. A compromise emerged with local authorities imposing means-tested charges, and National Assistance being made available to enable low-income people to meet part of the total cost of care. The division created a potential source of conflict between local and central government, as each would seek to minimize the cost falling upon it. Furthermore, after 1948 the local authorities were allowed to develop a variety of welfare services outside institutions – notably home helps and meals for the old or disabled. The charging policies they adopted for these often led to friction with the national relief agency.

Such disputes have not just occurred as a result of the way in which 'cash' and 'care' responsibilities were redistributed after the ending of the Poor Law. They have also arisen in relation to health services, child care services and education services. Some particularly intractable issues have arisen in relation to the last named services. These have been associated with the provision of cash grants to students by local authorities, means-tested school meals, and the availability of grants for school uniforms (Bull 1980).

What, then, have been the principal issues arising from the

existence of both national and local means testing? First, as we saw in the case of housing benefit, several of the local means-testing schemes were imposed upon local government by central government as a result of a concern to 'target' national subsidies. Such a situation placed central government under an obligation to secure uniformity of implementation, implying a control problem in which there was likely to be conflict between a desire for a unified system of rules and a need to ensure that the scheme could adapt to wide-ranging circumstances.

Second, where local schemes operated alongside national means tests, a range of issues arose about compatibility between schemes. To what extent could they treat similar administrative problems in the same way: providing for consistency of treatment of such issues as defining household composition; assessing the obligations of adult 'non-dependent' members of the household; interpreting the obligations of sexual partners to each other; and allowing for costs entailed in going to work? Accompanying these detailed administrative issues was a more general one: should the different means tests operate with similar 'scales' for assessing need? If they did, life was made much easier for administrators and claimants alike; acceptance of one benefit became a 'passport' to all and it was easier to learn entitlement rules. Furthermore, situations were avoided where different individuals found they were better off on different combinations of benefits. However, there was, and still is, a fundamental drawback to such compatibility: it creates a situation in which, just as a claim for one benefit can be a claim for all, a rise in income which disqualifies for one will disqualify for all and contribute to the 'poverty trap'.

Third, where both central and local government are involved in income maintenance, attempts will be made to shift costs onto each other. Thus, local government sees advantages in devising rules for their means tests which exclude the recipients of the general national benefits scheme for help. Central government responds to this either by refusing additional aid to claimants upon whom local authorities have imposed charges, thereby causing hardship, or by legislating to extend control over local discretion. Some of the battles over these issues, and the eventual compromises achieved, have imposed extensive administrative costs, both in the form of more complex rules and in the need for more elaborate liaison.

Fourth, the whole picture is further complicated where the benefits provided by local authorities have private sector equivalents. Here, there have been cases, for example, with home help services where income maintenance supplements have been available to pay for private, but not for public, care. The 1986 Social Security Act dealt with this problem by eliminating *all* such payments. However, this leaves an even more intractable issue – with similarities to the private rent issue – concerned with the private sector provision of residential care. This topic is examined in the next section.

SOCIAL SECURITY, PRIVATE RESIDENTIAL CARE AND COMMUNITY CARE

Whilst the care of the sick is the responsibility of the National Health Service, the social care of dependent groups who are not in need of relatively continuous medical attention comes under the local authority 'social services departments' (or, in Scotland, 'social work departments'). The social services departments have duties to provide residential accommodation for elderly and disabled people in need of intensive social care and also have duties to provide various forms of domiciliary support to people to help them to remain outside residential care. This alternative form of care is generally described as 'community care', and both central and local government have made efforts to extend it so that, wherever possible, it can render residential care unnecessary. Hence there is a complex, and hard to define, boundary between residential care and community care, with scope to extend the latter (generally cheaper) alternative if sophisticated packages of domiciliary services can be put together.

However, this is by no means the only ill-defined boundary. There is another between care provided by the health services and local authorities and a third important boundary lies between the responsibilities of social services and housing departments. Efforts by the latter in providing suitable housing, and in particular sheltered forms of housing, will be important to the operation of successful community care arrangements.

We have, then, a range of boundary issues, in which different authorities will be tempted by their own financial constraints to shift responsibilities across to others. There has been an earnest quest for administrative and financial arrangements between authorities which minimize these boundary conflicts and stimulate the establishment of rational care arrangements. However, the solution of some of these boundary problems has been complicated by the existence of a private care sector which is partly supported by public funds through the income maintenance system.

As this book is going to press these issues are all under review. The next few paragraphs therefore describe a system operating at the end of 1989 which will be changed soon after that. This is followed by a discussion of the expected changes, their rationale and possible consequences.

Individual charitable organizations or commercial enterprises may establish private residential care homes. If those homes provide regular nursing care they have to be registered by the health authority, and are subject to inspection from that source. If they provide general social, but not nursing, care they come under a similar social services department registration and inspection system. There are also homes requiring 'dual' registration from both authorities. All these homes obviously reduce the burden upon statutory care providers. While they make it easier for local authorities to maintain an adequate supply of residential places, they also create distortions in attempts to plan residential care provisions and may, in a sense, 'frustrate' the move towards community care by providing new residential resources for people deemed not to be in need of such care. Of course, it may be argued, why should this matter, is it not best to give people the choice between community and residential care? The reason it is regarded as a problem is that the public sector is paying for much of this care through means-tested benefits.

Individuals in private residential care may apply for income support. Their benefit level is determined by the amount by which charge for residential care, plus a small 'personal' cash allowance, exceeds their other income resources. The normal income support rules about capital obviously apply. Many low-income elderly people can thus get state help to pay for private residential care. Inevitably, however, the Department of Social Security imposes a limit to the charges it will meet. So the same issue arises as with high rents. This charge limit tends to determine charge levels in the private sector, except inasmuch as homes may use differential charging systems to obtain more from those of their occupants not in income support, and the relatives of those on income support may contribute to enable higher charges to be met.

Before 1980 the Department of Health and Social Security kept a tight limit on the charges they would meet. After this date, the rules were relaxed, and local social security office managers were given considerable discretion to accept higher charges. The subsequent dramatic growth of private sector homes placed the Conservative Secretary of State in a further dilemma between his commitment to the development of the private sector and his concern to keep income maintenance expenditure under control. His solution, in 1983, was to impose national limits. The standard limit set in April 1989 is £140 per week, but higher limits apply to the mentally handicapped and to the disabled elderly; and, for certain groups (the elderly disabled and terminally ill), the limit for a nursing home may be £235 per week.

A report by the 'watchdog' body set up by the government to carry out monitoring and 'value for money' studies on local expenditure on 'community care', the Audit Commission, talked of the 'perverse effects of social security policies' in this area of care. It pointed out that anyone entitled to means-tested benefit 'who chose to live in a residential home is entitled to allowances' up to the limit imposed by the benefit rules. It went on:

> In short, the more residential the care, the easier it is to obtain benefits, and the greater the size of payment. And Supplementary Benefit funding cannot be targeted towards those individuals most in need of residential care. Nor are homes judged on whether they are giving value for money within the category of care for which they are registered. (Audit Commission 1986: 44)

The Audit Commission team were very concerned about the extent to which this income maintenance subsidy of residential care distorted the pattern of care in the country as a whole. They noted the extent to which private homes are unevenly distributed geographically, commenting on their high incidence in the relatively prosperous southern and south-western parts of England. The consequence of this was, they said, that

> . . . while central government attempts to achieve equitable distribution of public funds across the country, through the use of complex

formulae within the National Health Service and local government, the effects can be largely offset by Supplementary Benefit payments for board and lodging. (Audit Commission 1986: 3)

A joint committee of civil servants and local government representatives reported on this issue in 1987. Their report (which will be described in short as the 'Firth Report' after the woman who chaired it) looked at the various alternative ways of rationalizing the mix of public and private residential care by bringing the subsidy of residents either all under local authority control or all under supplementary benefit control. They recommended the former. This would involve a transfer of resources to local government from the supplementary benefit system, and would put the local social services departments in a position to ration access to grants on the basis of need for care in the same way as they currently ration access to places in public sector homes.

After the Audit Commission report on community care, the government commissioned Sir Roy Griffiths to make recommendations on community care policies as a whole. He recommended (HMSO 1988) that there should be a system under which local authority social services departments decided on social – not income – grounds what care was necessary and then had a responsibility to ensure that individuals received that care, either from the public or private sector. If the individuals were then unable to pay the care costs from the standard benefits or from other income it would then be the responsibility of the local authority to provide a subsidy. In effect, Griffiths backed the Firth proposals, arguing for an appropriate transfer of funds from central to local government to allow for the changed responsibility. At the time of writing, the government has just announced that it proposes to accept Sir Roy Griffiths's proposals on this subject. This will mean that individuals in need of residential care will receive standard income support benefits, if they qualify for them, from the Department of Social Security and will similarly be able to get housing benefit for 'normal' housing costs; their additional 'care' costs will, however, be paid by the social services departments. Nevertheless, at the same time as the government sees local social services authorities becoming responsible for determining 'need' for residential care, and thus the rationer of any subsidy, it also proposes to ensure that the relative roles of those authorities as the direct providers of care will decline in favour of the private sector. In this sense local authorities will become the 'buyers' of packages of private care for low-income people, while their roles as suppliers of such care decline.

However, there are many complicated issues about care costs which this reform will have to handle. 'Care' does not only come in the form of comprehensive residential care. There are a variety of situations in which vulnerable individuals are given social support alongside the provision of accommodation. Young people who were in local authority care as children are often accommodated in hostels or lodgings where they receive some support. Mentally ill or handicapped people are often similarly found 'halfway' supported accommodation outside hospitals. In all these cases the government is moving towards a situation in which basic housing costs come under housing benefit, but support comes under social services departments. Since many of the care costs have hitherto been 'buried' within either income support arrangements or housing benefit, some complicated shifts of financial responsibility are involved. Given the splits at national level between the responsibilities of the different departments and at local level between different authorities, there are good grounds to fear that the so-called rationalization of this complex subject will result either in situations in which some individual problems are ignored (for example, the difficulties young people on very low income support scales will have on meeting the costs of board) or in situations in which the old game of seeking to shift responsibilities onto other authorities' budgets will be replayed in new forms.

On top of all this the government has made it clear that it wants local authorities to have to relate decisions about the rationing of residential care to decisions about community support in individuals' own homes (home helps, meals and so on), and that it wants the provision of both of these forms of care to be increasingly privatized. Local authorities will buy packages of care on behalf of needy people in their areas. It is not clear at this stage what policies will be developed to deal with issues either about charging consumers or about means testing to concentrate such charges on those able to pay. Clearly, however, there are quite likely to be three sets of means-testing policies here with social services means tests in addition to those for income support and housing benefit.

Readers will not, at this stage, need reminding of the complications which may follow.

CASH AND CARE: SOCIAL WORK AND INCOME MAINTENANCE

The problem of care costs leads the discussion nicely into a wider issue about interactions between social security policy and other areas of social policy, and also the relationship between publicly provided social work services (in the local authority social services and social work departments) and social security.

The abolition of the Poor Law, whilst leaving some income-related maintenance problems with local authorities, did seem to free the then embryonic social work profession, in a way which was not the case in many other countries, from responsibilities for income maintenance administration. But this did not resolve, for social workers, the problems of the relationship between help for families with non-material problems and help with material problems. On the one hand, to what extent do social security officers, charged with meeting material needs, have to concern themselves with (a) non-material needs (or problems) they might identify in the course of their visits or interviews, and (b) interactions between material and non-material needs (budgeting difficulties, family conflicts over money and so on)? On the other hand, to what extent should social workers concern themselves with material needs they encounter, and thus help families to budget, seek aid from charities, or, perhaps, pressure social security for more assistance? Hence, so far as the social security/social work interface was concerned, the issues at stake have concerned what Stevenson (1973) describes as 'the interaction of the different aspects of human need – material, social and psychological'. She continues:

> Social work is, by definition, concerned with these interactions and this concern gives it its distinctive character. To concentrate on any one to the exclusion of any other is to do violence to the person in need and to collude with those processes of fragmentation that are increasingly recognised as constituting a serious problem in complex urban societies. (Stevenson 1973: 29–30)

This problem, difficult enough in its own right, was made more complex in the 1960s. As social work, in what were then the Children's Departments, increasingly focused, in the 1950s and 1960s, on preventive work designed to support children in their own homes, social workers became more and more dissatisfied with the fact that they could not make cash payments themselves. Jean Packman describes the situation as follows:

> They experienced the frustration of recognising many family situations where cash or help in kind would greatly assist their preventive and rehabilitative efforts, yet there were no funds available for them to use. Some one-parent families would manage more comfortably if money could be given to them to make good day-care arrangements for their children while they worked. . . . There was no sanction for such direct help to families under the Children's Act so departments had to exercise their ingenuity by indirect means. They could act as persuasive go-between to the National Assistance Board for families where the parent was not in work. (Packman 1975: 60–1)

In 1963 the Children and Young Persons Act was passed, which altered this situation in England (slightly different later legislation had a similar impact in Scotland) by enabling local authorities to provide 'advice, guidance and assistance' to promote the welfare of children by diminishing the need to put them in care. The assistance could be 'in kind, or in exceptional circumstances, in cash'. When the Children's Departments were integrated into the more comprehensive social services departments in 1970 they took this power with them. The later Children Acts of 1980 and 1989 carried the power forward in the legislation.

In 1975 Peter Laing and myself (Hill and Laing 1979) examined how social services departments in England used their own money-giving powers under Section One of the Children and Young Persons Act. Were they using these powers to give help where central government was explicitly unable to provide benefits, as seemed to have been envisaged by those who advocated the original legislation? Or were they actually taking some of the pressure off the central means-testing scheme by making payments in situations in which that scheme could well have been considered to be responsible? A study of payments in London by Lister and Emmett (1976) suggested the latter conclusion. Our own research (Hill and Laing 1979) largely reinforced that view, as did similar research on the Scottish system (Valencia and Jackson 1979). Our findings were supported by later research indicating that this issue remained a live one in the 1980s (Stewart and Stewart 1986).

This problem has been given a new twist by the 1986 Social Security Act. Nowadays the income support system is much more rigid, with provisions for a response to exceptional and emergency situations through the cash-limited Social Fund and, in the majority of cases, in the form of a loan. This new situation is an obvious threat to the small budgets provided by local authorities for Section One payments. The local authorities do not want to find that these budgets have to grow rapidly to meet needs the Department of Social Security is now unprepared to meet (Jones 1989).

The position of local authority social workers is further complicated by assumptions made by the Department of Social Security (and embodied in the Social Fund guidelines for their staff) that social workers will cooperate in the assessment of need for Social Fund help, particularly in sorting out cases where community care grants will help people to leave, or remain out of, institutional care. The local authority associations, the main social workers' organization (British Association of Social Workers) and the principal local government trade union (NALGO) have all refused to accept the role the Department of Social Security have identified for social workers. A complicated policy of 'determined advocacy' has been adopted, in essence involving agreeing to help clients fight the Social Fund for the best possible deal (community care grants being the ideal) whilst not cooperating with the Social Fund to vet claims, sort out budgeting problems or weed out 'undeserving' claimants.

Social workers are in a difficult position. Most of their clients are dependent on state benefits. They acknowledge that clients' problems are complicated and exacerbated by poverty. Dealing with difficulties in obtaining benefits, needs for additional help and debt problems are only part of the social work task (Wilson and Hill 1988). Social workers have therefore been happy to delegate such work to welfare rights experts where they are available. However, because such experts are rare, social workers have often had to do the best they can, despite inadequate knowledge of benefits and with many other pressures on their time. Often involvement in such problems has been limited by the feelings of some social workers that it 'gets in the way of real social work'

(Hill and Laing 1979). The continually changing social security system has been bewildering. The latest changes, in the 1986 Act, seem to undermine a central aspect of welfare rights work, applying for single payments, but brings back local discretion (the Social Fund) with which many social workers felt comfortable in the past. Yet it is a very much less benign discretion – with loans and budget limits as its context. The official non-cooperation stance does offer a way to deal with the new situation, but it also provides an encouragement to the view that social workers must treat the material circumstances of their clients as something they can do nothing about. While some would call that getting back to 'real social work', others would view it as the ultimate encouragement to 'cop out' and disregard poverty's causal role in other social problems.

SOCIAL SECURITY AND EMPLOYMENT POLICY

Finally, in this discussion of social security interactions with other social policies, some comments are appropriate on employment policy. It is a matter for debate as to how central this issue is for social security as a whole. For many Marxist analysts of social policy it is very central:

> Throughout its [the social security system's] history its primary role has been to uphold the operation of a capitalist labour market, with its social and sexual divisions of labour, and to control and contain the inequalities and poverty that result. (Novak 1988)

It was suggested in Chapter 1 that this is a view which needs to be considered when we analyse the social security system. It is a view which clearly has its greatest plausibility when we look at the way the system of benefits for the unemployed is operated, and it is this which will be in full focus in this section, with the wider view as background (in harder or softer focus, according to personal ideology).

During the latter part of the nineteenth century it began to be widely recognized that unemployment was an evil that befell people through no fault of their own, an evil which individuals found it just as difficult to avoid as sickness, and therefore something with which a social security system might be legitimately concerned. Yet, in the course of the evolution of policies for the relief of unemployment, the view that this may have voluntary causes remained of determining importance for the system. Clearly there was some logical justification for this: unemployment is not so incontrovertible a 'condition' as old age and is not so outside the control of the individual as sickness. People do sometimes give up jobs needlessly and sometimes make little effort to get work once unemployed. But the relationship between voluntary and involuntary unemployment is a complicated one; the unemployed cannot be divided simply, by administrative fiat, into those who *cannot* work and those who *will not* work.

Nevertheless, policies towards the unemployed are a mixture of help and coercion which seems to be based upon an assumption that, whilst the majority of unemployed men can be given regular benefits and employment services, a minority can be fairly simply singled out for more coercive treatment. (I use the word 'men' deliberately: the system has been very much a system to deal with male unemployment; the treatment of women, with its strong emphasis upon limiting female access to the unemployment benefit system, has differed markedly – an issue to which we shall return.) The way the various policies interact tends to maximize the coercion and minimize the aid received by those amongst the unemployed who are least well equipped to compete in the labour market. In order to explain how this occurs, it is necessary to describe the principal procedures adopted by the system to deal with the unemployed.

It has already been observed that the unemployment benefit scheme is hedged around with rules which prevent individuals from procuring benefit if they have left work without good cause or have been sacked for 'misconduct'. It also allows for the stopping of benefit when individuals have refused suitable opportunities for work or for training. In addition, the Social Security Act 1989 makes it possible for unemployment benefit to be stopped where individuals are not actively seeking work. The draft regulations for this measure suggest that individuals will be likely to have their benefits stopped if they cannot provide evidence of job-seeking activities in the immediate past.

These, then, are the standard safeguards against the 'exploitation' of the unemployment benefit system. There are comparable rules relating to income support claimants. In this case, individuals do not lose all their benefit, but in practice have their benefits reduced below subsistence levels. This reduction is known as the 'voluntary employment deduction' which normally reduces income by 40 per cent of the personal allowance for a single claimant of their age.

It has been noted that most of these benefit disqualification rules date back to the early years of the scheme, although they have in practice been made more draconian in the recent past – indeed, in many respects, more draconian than some of the rules which operated in the 1930s (see Deacon 1976). During the years of very low unemployment, between the 1940s and the 1970s, the control rules within the system assumed comparatively little significance. It is a notable paradox that controls against the abuse of the system are more salient at times of job scarcity than at times when work is easy to get.

In the early 1970s the government decided that the employment service was far too clearly associated with the system of benefit. It decided that, if this service was to be an active force in the labour market of the time, its links with the unemployment benefit system should be largely weakened. A set of recommendations, produced by the government in 1971, *People and Jobs*, had this to say about the employment service:

> The Employment Service in its present form is not, however, able to grasp the opportunities which undoubtedly exist in a modern labour market. The majority of workers who register with the employment office are those claiming unemployment benefit. For this reason the service is regarded by many workers and employers as a service for the unemployed – and mainly for manual workers at that. . . . The task facing the Service is to break out of the situation where employers do not use it because they doubt – somewhat rightly – whether it has suitable people on its books and where workers seeking jobs do not visit the local employment office because vacancies they want are not notified by the employer. (Department of Employment 1971)

In accordance with this philosophy, during the 1970s the government developed a separate system of Job Centres, many of which were based in shops in the main shopping areas. There was a debate about whether the separate unemployment benefit offices should go over to Department of Health and Social Security control, but in practice they remained run by the Department of Employment on behalf of the Department of Health and Social Security. The Job Centres on the other hand, and the government's whole training system, were devolved to an organization called the Manpower Services Commission. One consequence of this devolution was that the Supplementary Benefits Commission increased the vigilance with which it sought to control its own claimants for benefit, recognizing that the employment system was comparatively uninterested in the operation of the control measures.

In the late 1980s that whole policy was totally reversed. The Manpower Services Commission has been abolished. A government publication in 1988 had this to say:

> Many of those who are genuinely unemployed have lost touch with the jobs market. That is why the separate management of the Job Centre network and the Unemployment Benefit Service no longer makes any sense. Over recent years, unemployed people have continued to attend benefit offices, but their contact with Job Centres has often been limited to occasional scrutiny of the self service displays. There has been no opportunity for Job Centre staff to advise them regularly and individually on the jobs, training and other opportunities available. *It is in no ones interest that unemployed people remain out of touch with the jobs market and become passive recipients of unemployment benefits.* (Department of Employment 1988: 28)

Hence the wheel has come full circle. But the change between the mid-1970s and the late 1980s has been more than an organizational change. A period of high unemployment has seen an increasing range of programmes targeted towards the unemployed, designed to take them off the unemployment registers and put them into various forms of work and training, or some combination of the two. Although it would not be appropriate here to go into all these developments in detail, it is important to note those programmes which interact significantly with the benefit system.

By 1988 after a complicated sequence of developments in employment creation and training programmes, two main central government programmes emerged: the Youth Training Scheme (YTS) for young people under eighteen and the Employment Training Scheme (ET) for people above that age. In the case of YTS the government ruled that young single people under eighteen should *normally* only get the allowance payable to participants in the Youth Training Scheme and should not qualify for any form of income support. Exceptions were allowed for certain groups of vulnerable young people without parental support. However, for the majority of young people, falling outside the specially protected groups, a refusal of a YTS place or departure from a YTS scheme or even (surprisingly) the unavailability of a local scheme, will be followed by unemployment in which no income maintenance is available of any kind. In this way the government has widened the original rule, which enabled them to stop benefit to people who refused suitable training offers, to embrace the whole of the potentially unemployed in the under-eighteen group.

The position with regard to over-eighteens is more complicated. The government first adopted a series of measures for scrutinizing the claims of unemployed people, and particularly longer-term unemployed people. Some claimants were clearly deterred by questions which required them to indicate that they were ready to take all kinds of work and to move in search of work. On top of this was added the Restart Programme involving interviews of all people unemployed over six months. These Restart interviews are described by the government as interviews at which unemployed people are invited to discuss the problems they face in their search for a job. Each is offered advice and information about the job training and other opportunities available. The aim, in every case, is to agree a course of practical action which will help the individual get back into work. Then, in summer 1988 the Employment Training (ET) scheme was introduced – a 12-month training programme targeted towards long-term unemployed people, particularly those in the 18–25 age bracket. The scheme is complicated, involving a combination of employment and training, with most of the employment opportunities in the private sector. Participants in ET secure ordinary income support benefit together with an enhancement of £10 per week. Some claimants can obtain a little more than this. Some single parents can get help of up to £50 per week for child care costs; travelling, accommodation and equipment costs may be met; and bonuses may be payable on completion of a programme. In the months during which the ET scheme was being planned the government suggested that it might be made compulsory. To date, it has not done so but, once again, the standard rules relating to disqualification for unemployment benefit and limitation of income support may be applied to people who refuse training opportunities under this scheme. At the time of writing, the scheme is too new for this eventuality to have been fully tested; overwhelmingly at present individuals are entering the scheme voluntarily, and with high hopes. Nevertheless the 1989 legislation seems to be further tightening the pressures upon unemployed people to make clearly demonstrable efforts to seek work.

Traditionally, the interests of labour, and their wage rates, were protected by a set of rules preventing individuals who were newly unemployed from being forced to take jobs below the skill and wage levels which had prevailed in their previous job. The measures which could be applied against those refusing suitable employment could not be applied if the individual could show that the employment was not suitable. It was the case that these rules required the unemployed to relax their job and wage requirements after a long period of unemployment. Now, this is required after only a short period out of work. In any case a period of high unemployment tends to undermine this form of protection. It is therefore much more clearly the case today that the pressures upon the unemployed to seek work operate as a form of labour market discipline, which is likely to have an overall downward pressure upon wages.

Before concluding this discussion it is necessary to examine some of the issues particularly relating to unemployed women. In the 1920s and 1930s one of the driving forces behind the development of regulations requiring unemployed people to demonstrate that they were genuinely seeking work was a desire to limit claims from married women. Then, as was shown in Chapter 3, the Beveridge scheme (while not preventing female participation in the unemployment scheme) was framed in such a way as to indicate that married women should normally be expected to be outside the labour market, and their husbands' dependants. They might continue to be insurance contributors on marriage, and could therefore get limited benefits when unemployed, but the scheme was designed to deter this. Much later legislation, in 1975, required all full-time and many part-time women workers (with exceptions for those already excused contributions) to be insurance contributors. But it did not provide for full equality for women because unemployed married women cannot normally claim dependants' additions for husbands and children. So far as means-tested benefits are concerned, the situation is, as we have seen, one in which couples' resources are aggregated. Married women may be the claimants of means-tested benefits, but they will find that their husbands' incomes are taken into account, and they will in fact be entirely disqualified from claiming income support if living with a man in full-time work. Briefly, therefore, married or cohabiting women may claim unemployment benefit as if they were single persons but cannot claim means-tested benefits in their own right.

Whilst that is the broad formal position so far as married and cohabiting women are concerned, in practice the government has encouraged unemployment benefit office staff to vet unemployment benefit claims from this group of women very thoroughly. The increased effort to ensure that people are actively seeking work, which was given statutory emphasis in the 1989 legislation, has been particularly directed towards this group of claimants. An unwillingness to travel away from a partner or to work unsocial hours, and any limitation upon availability for work posed by a need to solve child care problems, is likely to be used to disqualify or deter an insurance benefit claim from a married woman.

Single parents with dependent children – the majority of whom are female – may currently obtain income support without there being a requirement to register for work. The main problem for this group of claimants is that, as has already been pointed out, the ungenerous rules concerning part-time or occasional earnings tend to deter labour market participation. In the next few years we may see changes on this issue – the child care payment provisions in relation to the Employment Training scheme cited above are perhaps a 'straw in the wind'. Such changes may increase opportunities for single parents to supplement their benefit income, but they may also disadvantage them. At the time of writing, Ministers are showing an interest in ideas, originating from the USA (Murray 1984), on ways to try to use the benefit system to deter single parenthood. A 'workfare' system which, far from helping single parents to enhance their income, would force them into the low-paid end of the labour market would be a marked backward step for single parents in Britain, particularly female ones.

To summarize this section, we see, then, a variety of ways in which the support system for the unemployed is connected to labour market services and training in such a way that it will operate, as Marxist analysts have suggested, as a form of labour market discipline. But can this specific comment about the employment services be applied generally to social security? The Marxist argument sees social security as performing two functions, one of them being to maintain a reserve army of labour, at low levels of benefit, in readiness to move into the labour market when they are needed. The second wing of the Marxist analysis of social security sees the system very much more in terms of its role in legitimizing the existing system. The existence of adequate sickness benefits and pensions schemes helps to prevent general dissatisfaction with the capitalist status quo.

It has to be recognized that the two functions suggest very different roles for social security. Furthermore, the second function – the protection of individuals who are sick, old or young – can in some respects be seen as a policy which actually helps to keep them off the labour market, to prevent them from competing with other workers. In this sense, social security may be seen as a concession to the interests of labour, and not as something that contributes to the maintenance of a reserve army of labour and low wage levels. Similar observations may apply to benefits for families, and particularly for single parents. If the aim of the British system was principally to ensure that these categories of individuals, particularly women, would be ready as a reserve army of labour, it would operate in a way very much more like the American scheme of Aid to Families of Dependent Children (AFDC) which applies very strong pressures upon single parents to enter the labour market. By contrast, the British system, with its poor disregards for part-time work, and its disincentives to participation in the labour market at low levels of income, must at present be seen as a system which tends to keep such individuals out of, rather than in, the labour market.

CONCLUSION

Chapter 7 discussed some considerations about policy implementation which are relevant to the evaluation of current policy, and the examination of alternative policy options. This chapter has looked at a variety of other issues about the way social security is put into practice, where interactions with other policy areas are relevant. As was suggested in the brief introductory section, in which the example of transport policy was used to show the variety of ways in which considerations about protecting individuals from costs or enhancing their incomes might produce complex interactions between social security policy and other policies, both policy-making and implementation in this field are affected by relationships with other policy areas.

The chapter has focused on four areas where social security policy interacts with other policies: housing, residential and community care, social work and employment. It is interesting to compare the forms these interactions take. In the case of housing policy the long-standing problems for social security about how to take into account housing costs, together with a shift of government policies away from the relatively indiscriminate subsidy of rented housing towards focused subsidy based on individual needs, has made the interaction between the two policy areas very significant for both areas. Such interactions remain inevitable so long as (a) the social security system lacks benefits high enough to make it unnecessary to take into account actual housing costs (as was Beveridge's ideal for an insurance-based system), and (b) the housing policy system restricts general subsidies, other than mortgage interest relief to owner-occupiers. It is, of course, the developments on the housing side that have been crucial for the recent developments in this interaction in Britain. Mortgage interest subsidies are not means-related, nor were general subsidies for council houses or measures which depressed the levels of private sector rents. It is the shift away from all these measures (except, of course, mortgage interest subsidies) towards means-related subsidies which have made the interaction between housing and social security policy such an important and complex issue. It might be added, incidentally, that if mortgage interest relief were abolished this would increase costs for the social security system and if it, too, were 'targeted' towards lower-income people that could add yet another complication for means testing.

When, in the final chapter, we look at alternative models for the social security system we will also find the housing cost issue as a source of difficulties for some of the more simplistic approaches to reform.

Some of the same issues arise in the interactions between social security and social care, if for no other reason than that housing cost issues are intertwined with the latter. However, these interactions bring into sharp focus some of the issues about social benefits 'in kind'. Two alternative models of social policy, generally associated with opposite ends of the political spectrum, offer ways of eliminating most of the awkward questions about interactions between social security and social care policy. One such model involves the suggestion that social services of this sort should be free and universally available to anyone in need of them, regardless of income. The other model suggests that market prices should be charged for these services, with the implication that inability to pay on account of income deficiency should be of no concern to the social care system *per se*. The fact is that, in the real world of political choices, options are adopted between these two extremes, with both resources and need being used as rationing criteria, thereby creating the kind of interaction between policy sectors discussed in this chapter.

The third area of policy interaction, between social security and social work, is at least in part a consequence of the interaction in relation to social care, because of the close connections between social care and social work. However, there is more to it than this. As Stevenson (1973) has shown, the special feature of the approach to the provision of 'last resort', means-tested, benefits adopted in Britain on the abolition of the Poor Law was to leave social workers out of the income – maintenance decision process. This feature of the British system makes it different from that adopted in many other developed countries. There are good arguments for this separation of income – maintenance and social work (see Handler 1973; Jordan 1974). However, inasmuch as benefits are inadequate and inasmuch as there are opportunities for outside advocates to pressure the system for more help for individuals, social workers are likely to want to engage with the system on behalf of their poor clients. Whilst in the first two examples of policy sector interaction discussed above there are clear reasons why policy-makers and implementers *on both sides* will want to negotiate with the other, in this case we have an interaction where there is little basis for an exchange relationship. Social workers want things, on behalf of their clients, from social security officers, but the latter generally want nothing in exchange, apart from the reduction in the conflict which may arise over the decisions. This unequal 'exchange' relationship has been analysed interestingly by Leach (1981) and by Hvinden (1989).

Finally, our fourth case displays more or less the opposite extreme to our third case. So far as social security support for the unemployed is concerned, issues about the working of the labour market are of fundamental importance in determining the system's character and day-to-day functioning. That point has been put very strongly by Marxist writers. Whether or not we agree with their analyses it would be naive not to recognize how closely policies on the unemployed and benefits for the unemployed are interrelated. But it is not merely unemployment benefit policies which interact with employment policies. Imagine how different our labour market would be in the absence of state pensions. Bear in mind that British benefit policies for single-parent families reduce labour market participation by the heads of those families. The same can be said of the benefits for the sick and disabled. Overall, as economic analyses remind us, the social security system involves massive transfers of resources between individuals with consequent complex effects upon economic behaviour. This is an appropriate note on which to end this penultimate chapter and move on to a final look at the British system as a whole.

9. What Future for Social Security?

INTRODUCTION

This chapter will be divided into two halves. The first half, containing two subsections, will look at the characteristics of the British social security system and offer some assessment of its adequacy. The first major section examines general questions about the adequacy of coverage of the whole system. This will be followed by a subsection which will return to, and summarize, the recurrent question of this book 'Is the Beveridge design still relevant?' The second subsection of this first half will develop further the analysis of that question by looking at an issue which is fundamental to it – namely, the way the system treats families and women in particular.

The second half of the chapter will review alternatives to the existing system. It will look at the arguments about negative income tax and about 'basic income' or 'social dividend'. It will also examine the sorts of suggestions that have been made for improving upon the basic Beveridge design, and in particular about the idea of a system based upon the Beveridge design without the insurance principle or the family assumption, and with better provisions for the disabled.

THE ADEQUACY OF COVERAGE

Obviously, the central issue about the level of the adequacy of the British social security system must be the extent to which the level of benefits available is sufficient for the relief of poverty. However, in practice, this is a very difficult question to answer. There is in Britain no official poverty line, and there has been a tendency to treat the minimum benefit level (that is now the income support level) as the definition of the poverty line. In addition, many students of poverty have gone beyond that to suggest that it is appropriate to define the poverty line as the income support level plus 30 or 40 per cent (Abel-Smith and Townsend 1965; Townsend 1979).

Spokespeople for the government have justifiably protested that the use of the benefit level as the definition of the poverty line, or worse still as the definition of a level substantially below the poverty line, creates a situation in which any steps taken by the government to improve benefit levels will have the effect of increasing the numbers defined as being in poverty. This protest would carry more weight if there had been some official attempt to identify an alternative line, or if there was clear evidence that the benefit levels had been set in a way that ensured that they were adequately above a poverty line. In fact there has never been any realistic attempt to relate benefit levels to minimum standards of living. The determination of the original National Assistance scales in 1948 was influenced by Rowntree's studies of poverty, and his effort to define a poverty line. Nevertheless, it is important to note, as Veit-Wilson (1986) has shown, that Rowntree himself recognized difficulties with his poverty line. He used a very severe definition of primary poverty, not because he believed that this could be seen as an adequate national minimum, but because it enabled him to show, at least at the time of his first study in 1899, that there were substantial numbers of people below even the most stringent poverty levels. He accompanied his concept of primary poverty with one of secondary poverty, recognizing that, unless individuals were exemplary managers of their own budgets and had no 'bad habits', they would be in fairly severe poverty with incomes quite significantly above his primary line. Hence, the use of the Rowntree primary line as the starting-point for the British social security scales cannot inspire any confidence in them as levels satisfactorily above a basic poverty level.

The process of uprating benefits since 1948 has been an erratic one. Between the 1940s and the 1970s uprating decisions were essentially ad hoc. Political judgements were made periodically about the uprating of benefits, obviously taking into account movements in wage levels and standards of living. In real terms, overall benefit levels were raised slightly from their 1940s levels, but these rises were insignificant in a society in which standards of living and expectations about the qualify of life were increasing rapidly. Since 1972 uprating of insurance benefits has at least been an annual process and there has been a tendency for the supplementary benefit/income support levels to move in line with price inflation. Even this has been a rather erratic process however, with adjustments being made at some points in the definition of the retail price index used for defining inflation for these purposes, and, again, some ad hoc decisions being taken designed to reduce the levels of social security rises (see p. 57).

If the official approach to the definition of poverty and the determination of the levels of benefit offers us little help in making a judgement about the adequacy of benefits, can we then get help from independent studies? Perhaps the two most influential independent studies carried out in Britain in recent years were the large study carried out by Peter Townsend in 1968–69 (Townsend 1979) and a study carried out by Mack and Lansley in 1983 (Mack and Lansley 1985). Both of these studies rejected Rowntree's approach and made no attempt to work out a standard for the measurement of poverty which would be based upon some idea of the minimum amount adequate to sustain life. The writers were only too well aware of the difficulties in doing this, pointing out that even Rowntree found it difficult to isolate his view about an adequate diet from some of the customs and practices in the society he was studying. These writers argue that one must recognize, in studying poverty within any one society, that standards regarded as minimal will depend upon customs and behaviour which are typical of that society. They argue that the poor will be identified, therefore, by an inadequacy of income which prevents them from sharing the normal customs and social practices of their society. Thus, in designing their studies, these writers sought to develop measures based upon evidence of incapacity to share in common forms of social behaviour. Townsend devised his own index to identify how, below a certain level of income, individuals could be shown by statistical analysis to be very unlikely to enjoy a variety of social conditions and forms of social life which were common in the society. Mack and Lansley developed Townsend's approach further and avoided the subjectivity of some of Townsend's judgements, by starting from a public opinion survey in which they sought to obtain a random sample of citizens to identify the possessions and amenities which they regarded as necessary. They could then devise an index of necessities and show the extent to which there were individuals in our society without these necessities. Again, there are some methodological problems with this approach, since amongst a group of people unable to afford the identified necessities there are of course individuals who have chosen not to avail themselves of them. However, this is not a problem when aggregate data, based upon a large sample survey, are considered.

It is argued, from both surveys, that there is substantial poverty in Britain. Furthermore, the data suggest that individuals who are forced to live upon minimal levels determined by the state means-tested benefits can, in general terms, be defined as being in poverty, as can also significant numbers of people with incomes only slightly above the benefit levels. In other words, these two independent studies of poverty both provide evidence to support the convention of fixing a poverty line at the level of 30 or 40 per cent above the state benefit level.

Nevertheless, these studies evidently provide no conclusive answer as to the definition of poverty. Defenders of the government, and right-wing critics of the generosity of the welfare state, have still found it possible to argue that the state benefit levels are more than adequate, that the Townsend and Mack and Lansley studies exaggerate poverty, and that the only realistic definition of poverty is to be literally starving (Joseph and Sumption 1979). Perhaps the strongest evidence against that severe view lies in the important studies on inequalities in health (Townsend and Davidson 1982; Whitehead 1988). These show that there is a very distinct correlation between income and health, so that, even if we use the most rigorous definition of ill-heath – that is, the likelihood of dying earlier – we find substantial differences between income groups within Britain. This suggests that we might develop an operational definition of poverty based upon the likelihood that individuals in poverty will live less long than others. Indeed, there can hardly be any more absolute concept of deprivation than this. Thus, if this line of argument is followed, it can be suggested that there is a serious problem of poverty, and that it might be appropriate to place the cut-off point between the 'poor' and 'non-poor' somewhere quite high up the income distribution, given that there is a difference in life expectancy running throughout that distribution.

We see, then, that the most central question about the adequacy of our benefit system is very difficult to answer. There are, however, secondary questions about the adequacy of the system for all groups in society. Are there particular groups of people who are *either* entirely deprived of even these basic state benefits *or* are paid benefits at levels markedly inferior to anyone else? In theory the British system's coverage is comprehensive. All individuals who are not in full-time work are able to apply for income support, and there is now also a substantial and complex group of benefits available for individuals in full-time work. In practice, measures taken to deter claims for benefit do leave some individuals outside the benefit system. We have noted earlier in the book that individuals who are deemed to have lost jobs through their own fault, or to have failed to have made sufficient efforts to find work, may have their unemployment benefit stopped and their income support reduced. For single people these measures may be more draconian and benefits may be stopped altogether. Under legislation passed in 1988 some 16 and 17 year-olds may be denied benefit. It may be suggested moreover that a variety of measures currently adopted against the unemployed have the effect of deterring claims to benefit altogether. We have similarly observed that there is a take-up problem amongst low wage-earners, so that, again, there exist some people who are nominally in full-time work, but who in practice are subsisting on very low income levels.

The system has also been structured in a way which allows higher levels of benefit for some groups of people than others. In particular, the income support system is now organized in a way which discriminates against the young, and to a lesser extent against all the unemployed. The provisions for single people under 25 have been based upon an assumption that individuals in this group will not normally form independent households. In a society in which many people become independent soon after leaving school, and the most notable evidence for this is the very strong tendency for individuals to leave home to seek higher education at the age of 18, this is an assumption which is out of line with everyday experience. There are therefore significant numbers of young people trying to maintain independent lives on benefits which are very inadequate in this respect. There are also some more complicated, but related, problems about the housing benefit availability for young people, particularly young people in board and lodging arrangements and hostels. So it seems reasonable to suggest that, whilst it is difficult to develop absolute measures to facilitate identification of the problem, there are some groups of people, particularly amongst the young, who may be said to be more clearly in poverty than others.

Whilst we may identify some groups of people for whom benefit provision is minimal, we must not forget that there are other groups which, although appearing to receive quite substantial benefit provisions, have such high needs that, in practice, the system is inadequate. It was shown earlier in the book that the changes which came with the introduction of the income support scheme involved assumptions that the scales would make additions for special needs unnecessary and that most extra, single, payments could be in the form of loans. Clearly, if the groups who had been high recipients of the various additions and single payments in the past were people characterized by high needs rather than extravagant behaviour, then the losses of these additional forms of help will have deepened their poverty. The evidence suggests that the people who will have suffered particularly badly from these changes will have been people in large families who have been dependent upon benefits for a long time. We recognize, at the same time, that the unemployed are treated rather worse than others by the system and we may identify the long-term unemployed as a group particularly likely to be in deep poverty.

There are also clearly a variety of problems, some of which have been discussed already, about the nature of the provision for the disabled in Britain. Again the simplification of the income support system has resulted in the system not responding in as sophisticated a way as it did previously to the needs of severely ill and disabled people on income support who have very high costs – for example, for special diets or the replacement of bedding. There is also here a more general issue about provision for the disabled, which lies in the relatively low levels of benefits to cover the cost of care. Attendance allowance clearly does not pay for attendance, and the additional benefits for carers do not, as has already been shown, pay for the costs of carers who have no other income. We may therefore identify amongst the disabled a group of people who appear to receive high benefits which are, in fact, low for their exceptionally expensive needs.

The Beveridge Design Today

This book has shown that, whilst Beveridge envisaged a system in which the normal social security provision should be funded by insurance benefits with the means test 'safety net' available only in exceptional cases, we have today a situation in which insurance has been weakened and the safety net is much more in evidence. Beveridge certainly always envisaged that the insurance benefits should be at a fairly minimal level. He saw this as a virtue, designed to encourage individuals to make private and voluntary provisions to ensure them incomes above 'state minimum' level. Manifestly, many individuals do this, particularly in the field of pension provisions. However, there are clearly great social variations in the feasibility of making separate individual provision, and, furthermore, those people who are most likely to have income maintenance problems during their working life – due to sickness, unemployment or caring responsibilities – are those who will find it most difficult to make independent provision for their old age. Obviously, very large numbers of insurance beneficiaries have not been in a good position to make independent provision to supplement those benefits, neither has a steadily growing and significant group of people whose needs stem from something which the state does not offer insurance against – family breakdown. This gives a substantial group of people who are either dependent upon basic insurance benefits or have no insurance entitlement at all. Furthermore, amongst the first group there are significant numbers for whom the insurance system is not adequate to lift them above the levels of need for means-tested benefits, either because of the continual failure to solve the problem of housing costs in the context of the insurance system, or because governments have tended to keep the insurance benefit levels very close to the qualifying levels for the means-tested benefits. Some examples of the interactions between insurance and means-tested benefit were provided in Chapter 6.

Overall social security in Britain may be defined in terms of the existence of three distinct 'classes' identifiable, not in conventional social class terms, but in terms of 'social divisions of welfare' (Titmuss 1958: ch. 2; Sinfield 1978; Rose 1981).

The first of these classes are people whose welfare, when out of employment, does not really depend on the social security system at all. They probably will draw insurance benefit, but it is private arrangements which are crucial to their well-being. When elderly, they will draw upon substantial private pensions and, when sick, their employers will supplement statutory sick pay, often making their salaries up to their normal levels. Unemployment will be rare for this group, and if it does occur it will be short and its impact will be cushioned by redundancy payments and severance pay. Women in this group may be dependent on male breadwinners, and their security in the event of family breakdown may depend upon post-marital financial settlements. Some women in this group may accordingly be vulnerable to a shift in circumstances which will abruptly 'demote' them from the first of the three classes into the third.

The second of the classes will be people for whom the insurance system still has some viability. When elderly they will, as a consequence of a lifetime of regular employment, be able to draw upon a National Insurance pension with earnings-related supplements. In the event of temporary sickness they will get statutory sick pay, and invalidity benefit may be satisfactory for longer terms of sickness so long as the problem is not too prolonged or too disabling. Spells of unemployment will also not be unduly frequent or prolonged, and again lump sum redundancy payments may provide help to supplement unemployment benefit. The only means-tested benefit the members of this class will be quite likely to encounter is housing benefit, when other resources are lacking to supplement insurance benefit. This class is, in a sense, the traditional working class in a fully employed society – the class for whom it may be argued the insurance system was designed. Our answer to the question about the viability of the Beveridge model must therefore depend to a considerable degree on the extent to which this moderately well-paid group, with reasonably secure jobs, continues to exist in our society. Prolonged unemployment or prolonged sickness readily 'demotes' people from this class into the third one. And what about female members of this class? We have already seen how their position in the system has been defined in terms of a 'dependent' relationship to male breadwinners. Where they are today both still secure in that 'traditional' situation, and also earners in their own right, their work situations, and sometimes their benefits, will help to keep their family unit safely in this class. Where this is not the case, on the other hand, 'demotion' comes even more surely than it does to their sisters in class one.

The third class can be defined in terms of what has been said about the two 'higher' classes. When elderly their insurance pension entitlement will be basic, or if working life has been severely interrupted, worse than basic. When sick, their employers will seldom allow them more than the basic statutory sick pay, and may well find ways to terminate their employment. They are a group for whom sickness will, in any case, be more likely to be prolonged. The same can be said about unemployment. When in employment their wages will be low, when out of work it will be hard to get back in (see Sinfield 1981). The breakdown of a relationship will bring immediate income maintenance problems for women. Overall, then, dependence on means-tested benefits is the lot of this group, probably both in and out of work. We are talking here, as suggested above, of this class as a class into which people may fall. But we must also remember that this class encounters a variety of vicious circles which reinforces their position once in it. In work, they experience the 'poverty trap'. Out of work, their deprivation brings cumulative disadvantages: greater vulnerability to sickness, difficulties in gaining access to new work opportunities, and ultimately an impoverished old age as a direct consequence of having had an impoverished youth and middle age.

In analysing the system in terms of this social divisions model, taking into account changes in our society which have made unemployment and family instability more pervasive than Beveridge anticipated, we can see how means tests have become much more important than Beveridge intended them to be. The irony of the situation is, furthermore, that the pervasiveness of the means tests tends to undermine the insurance principle. One may contrast here, for example, a man who has had a steady work record for a long period of time who then experiences a long spell of unemployment with a man who has contrived to live more or less outside the regular labour market. The second man might be, for example, someone whose working life has consisted of a mixture of hidden economy and illegal activities perhaps interspersed with periods in prison. The first man finds that the insurance benefits for which he has contributed provide him with insufficient insurance benefit for him to avoid applying for means-tested benefits to supplement his unemployment insurance. Furthermore, his unemployment benefit is exhausted after one year. The second man has little or no entitlement to insurance benefit but achieves much the same income as the first man. The first man can rightly complain that he has in effect contributed for nothing.

We will see later in this chapter how the logic outlined here has led some advocates of social security change to argue that the insurance system should be swept away altogether and replaced with a universal means-tested system. Meanwhile, that end is being approached by the government by incremental steps, as it allows the insurance system to deteriorate and places more emphasis upon the development of the means tests. This interacts critically with other social and economic changes.

Thus, we see that Britain has a system now in which means tests are of enormous importance. Earlier in the book the key weaknesses of means tests were identified as follows:

1. the tendency for underclaiming of entitlement;
2. the related problem of stigma;
3. the problem of the poverty trap.

Alternatives for reform of the system each profess to attack these problems, offering either better ways of means testing or ways of avoiding means testing. The search for better means testing is inevitably complicated by a tension between the need for simplicity on the one hand, to enable people to identify their entitlement and to get it with ease, and the need for effective targeting, which requires means tests to be elaborately adjusted to special circumstances but causes them to be correspondingly complicated – issues which will be covered later.

Social Security and the Family

We have seen that the British social security system is based upon the idea that the claiming unit is the nuclear family. Our system emerged out of the Poor Law, in which originally the claiming unit was the extended family. Some vestiges of assumptions about the extended family remain and are most evident in the assumptions about the extent to which adult non-dependent members of households should be expected to be contributors to the rents paid by the claimant members of the household, and in some of the assumptions made about the care of the elderly and disabled. However, in general, the system may be described as treating the nuclear family as the claiming unit: assuming that the claimant makes a claim which includes the needs for his or her spouse and their dependent children. Accordingly this also implies that, in any means test, the resources of these other individuals are also taken into account. This proposition has been put in sexually neutral terms but of course, traditionally, the concept was of a male claimant with a female dependent wife. The social security system has also found it necessary to define unmarried sexual partners as if they were married couples. The determination of benefit levels within the system is based upon an assumption that two people living together live more cheaply than two people living independently. For example in 1989–90 the unemployment benefit rate for a single person is £34.70 with £21.40 added for a 'spouse', while the income support rate for a single person over 25 is £34.90 with the corresponding rate for a couple of £54.40. The 'couple' rates are approximately 162 per cent and 167 per cent of the single rates in these two examples.

Beveridge's original design for social security has been defended as one that was developed at a time when marriage was very much more the mode and female labour market participation was very low. From some viewpoints, Beveridge might be portrayed as being generous towards women in making provision for dependants' benefits and widows' benefits based upon men's insurance contributions. He might have devised a system that was based simply upon the idea of individual contributions without dependants' additions, as had existed in the very early years of the British system and in the early years of the American system (see Achenbaum (1986) who carefully analyses the pros and cons of the two alternatives in the American system). This line of argument suggests that it is merely social changes that have made the Beveridge design irrelevant. An alternative view is that, even in Beveridge's time, women's interests and women's poverty problems were disregarded. Focus upon the family as the unit of study when the problems of poverty have been examined has tended to obscure female poverty (Millar and Glendinning 1989; Glendinning and Millar 1987). Even in Beveridge's time, single women were more likely to be poor than single men, and if the numbers of people in poverty, as opposed to the numbers of families in poverty, had been counted then, women would have far exceeded men. Furthermore, any approach to the study of poverty which examines issues about family resources tends to pay no attention to questions about the way resources are distributed within the family. Qualitative evidence suggests that women have tended to be the most deprived within poor families, less likely to take 'pocket money' for themselves for small pleasures and more likely to make sacrifices when the family encounters a specific budgeting problem. In other words, even though it is fair to argue that Beveridge could not have foreseen the dramatic change in the roles of women in our society, he could have given more attention to the extent of poverty among women in his own time.

However, if we then take both new evidence about female poverty and the changed status of women, and also the changed character of the family into account in looking at our social security system today, we must surely find that there is cause for disquiet about the continuation of the traditional family assumptions within the benefit system. There are several problems about the use of the family assumption in social security today. So far as insurance is concerned, the family assumption creates yet another example of a situation in which individuals pay substantial contributions for *de facto* minimal benefits. The working man earns an insurance pension with an addition for a dependent wife. If his wife is herself an earner she earns a single person's pension. However, that single person's pension is not additional to the dependants' pension; it replaces it. In practice, therefore, her insurance contributions may be said to earn a very much lower pension than would a single person's. It should also be noted that the provisions for widow's benefits are not mirrored on the other side of the sexual divide by a system of benefits for widowers. There are similar complications about the provisions for children within the benefit system.

So far as the means-tested benefits are concerned, the central problem about the family assumption has been the existence of rules to enable social security officials to treat unmarried sexual partners the same way as married ones. This has led to a variety of situations in which women claimants for benefit have been subject to investigation and harassment wherever they have been suspected of having male partners. They have accordingly been placed in very difficult situations when in extremely insecure sexual relations, or in situations in which they have been taken into houses occupied by men without there being any sexual relationship. The whole picture is further complicated by the fact that, where there are unstable sexual relationships, there are likely to be situations in which the men whom the system expects to be responsible for the care of women have other commitments to other women outside their current households.

Yet it is difficult to remove the traditional family assumption from the system. If, for example, changes were adopted which reverted to the earlier assumption that insurance benefits should be assessed on an individual basis, taking into account that women are now very much more likely to be insurance contributors, then the consequences would be:

1. that the needs of a minority of married women who have remained largely outside the labour force would be disregarded;
2. that women would be disadvantaged by the system's failure to take into account both their weaker position in the labour market as a whole and their lower earnings levels;
3. that no attention would be paid to the fact that, in our society, it is women who are most likely to break periods of employment to take on caring tasks, either of children or of ageing and disabled relatives, unless there was also an elaborate system of 'credits' for carers.

In other words were a more wholehearted insurance system developed to deal with this problem it would be necessary to consider greatly extending the case for insurance credits for periods devoted to caring tasks, or indeed to housework in general. An alternative way to deal with this problem would be to treat couples as 'earning units' and to divide the benefit from contributions evenly between them in assessing payments. Even this, however, would raise difficulties in cases of household splits unless the 'two can live more cheaply than one' assumption was also abandoned. Other ways of dealing with the problem are open to the objection that they would be expensive to the Exchequer. If, for example, the family assumption were to be abandoned in the assessment of means-tested benefits, the women without resources would consequently be able to claim benefits regardless of their spouses' income levels. Whilst this may be a defensible principle, it would be enormously costly. The combined problems for women of both insurance and means-tested assistance, and the difficulties in devising incremental changes to deal with them, offer an incentive to look for radically different ways of designing the British social security system. This is the subject of the next part of this chapter.

ALTERNATIVES FOR THE SOCIAL SECURITY SYSTEM

The two principal kinds of models which are offered as radical alternatives to the present British system are *negative income tax* and *basic income* (also known as 'social dividend'). The main exponents of the former are Minford (1984) and M. and R. Friedman (1981), whilst the latter is effectively advocated by Parker (1989), Walter (1988) and Jordan (1985, 1987). There is a variety of other models which are hybrids of the two approaches (for example, Meade 1978 and Dilnot, Kay and Morris 1984) and some writers (see Prest and Barr 1986) have professed to see little to distinguish between the two approaches. The issues about these two models can best be illustrated by a graphical presentation. Let us take as our starting-point an imaginary world in which there is neither taxation nor benefits. The relationship between every individual's gross income and their net income would be as set out in Figure 9.1. We see here a situation in which at any point on the income distribution the individual's gross income will be exactly equal to net income. In the real world, benefits increase net income and taxation or social security contributions reduce it. If the aim of the system was to totally equalize income by these methods, then the net effect of these two would be to tilt the line to the horizontal. In the real world, of course, taxation would exist even if there was no social security system. But taxation could be imposed in such a way that no attempt was made to dip the line towards the horizontal – that is, it could be equally onerous, regardless of the level of income (like a poll tax!) In practice most taxes are, to a greater or lesser degree, redistributive in their own

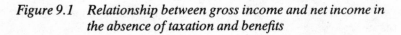

*Figure 9.1   Relationship between gross income and net income in
the absence of taxation and benefits*

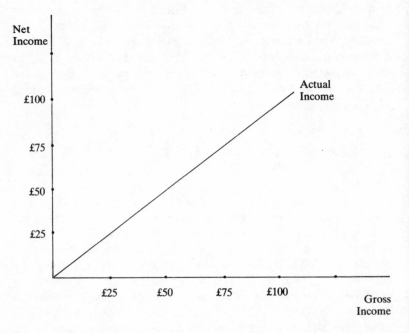

right. Social security is more explicitly redistributive. So, in reality, people with low gross incomes will tend to receive benefits and people with higher gross incomes will tend to pay tax.

Even here it is important to note that two very different redistributive principles may operate. The object may be merely to redistribute across any specific individual's lifetime. Arguments for insurance may be expressed in these terms, involving simply a concern that individuals provide for periods in their life in which earned income is unavailable. Social insurance goes a stage further than this involving, as we have seen, some pooling of risks and therefore some degree of redistribution. But it is also possible to see social security in much more explicitly redistributive terms, as making a deliberate attempt to shift the distribution of incomes towards equality.

However, the above is far more rational than the reality of tax and social security in our society. The fact of the matter is that many individuals will be simultaneously both the payers of tax and social security contributions and the recipients of social security benefits. The actual way the line representing the relationship between gross income and net income may be drawn will be affected by some quite complicated transfers.

The core point within the argument for negative income tax is an attack upon that irrationality. The exponents of negative income tax argue that it is inefficient for the state to be both giving and taking away from the same individuals. They argue that it is particularly inefficient that state benefits should be going to individuals with large earned incomes. Individuals in this school of thought have particularly criticized the child benefit as an indiscriminate benefit in these terms. By demonstrating the relationship between net income and gross income, Figure 9.2 illustrates the way advocates of negative income tax would like to redesign the system by providing a unified tax–benefit system

Figure 9.2   *Relationship between gross income and net income with a unified tax–benefit system (negative income tax)*

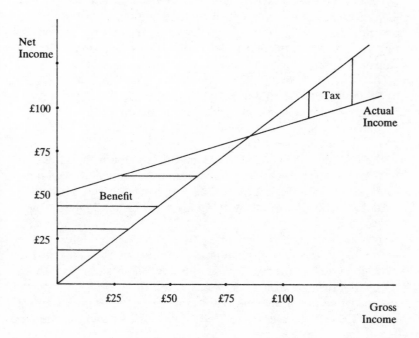

which uses one and the same means test to determine benefit for low-income people and tax for higher-income people. Below a certain threshold, people would be benefit recipients; above it they would be taxpayers. Almost all the complexities described in this book would, allegedly, be swept away. The very simplest arguments for negative income tax advocate a guaranteed weekly minimum up to a certain point. They would, to use an arbitrary example, perhaps guarantee incomes up to say £50. The consequence would be a line drawn on Figure 9.2 across horizontally from the £50 net income point until it hits the diagonal. However, most advocates of negative income tax recognize that this would be problematical in that there would be no incentive to earn if one were below the threshold. Someone with earned income of £50 would, in effect, get no return for work as that amount would be guaranteed anyway. They are therefore likely instead to argue for the tapering off of this benefit as shown in the diagram.

Negative income tax offers us, therefore, what seems to be a very rational model for the redistribution of incomes. Low earners secure state benefits, which taper off until, at a certain point, they start to become taxpayers. One institution administers both tax and benefits. What then are the problems about this proposal? The central problem is the familiar poverty trap. Any system of negative tax needs to come to terms with the complicated relationship between

a) the absolute minimum income guaranteed;
b) the negative income tax withdrawal rate; and
c) the tax rate.

If the scheme is to start with a generous minimum then the cost of that minimum has to be paid either in a steep withdrawal rate, and therefore a high poverty trap problem, or in a shallow withdrawal rate followed by steep tax rates on the higher ranges of income.

The second problem with negative income tax relates to the definition of the state minimum. We have already seen that the existing systems do not operate with any single minimum: there are variations according to family size; there are the income support premiums; and there are a variety of other adjustments for special cases, such as disabled people. If negative income tax had similar complications built into it, then much of its initial simplicity would be lost. It would have a variety of minimum points for benefit and a variety of tapers operating away from that point. You would need detailed enquiries in order to determine individual entitlements and these could be perhaps every bit as complicated as our existing range of social security investigations. All these complications need to be related to the fact that in Britain the individual tax codes are currently determined on an annual basis, whilst social security benefits are determined on a weekly basis. It would be quite impossible to operate a sophisticated system of income support for low-income people on an annual basis, since it would cause far too much hardship for those low-income individuals who commonly experience short-term income fluctuations. The tax system would therefore have to be adjusted to take into account this need for weekly changes, and it is this sort of change which has been resisted by tax administrations. Whilst such administrative conservatism could be brushed aside, it must be recognized that it would be no simple task to adjust the tax system to enable it to operate in this way.

Another feature of much of the work on negative income tax is that little attention has been given to a problem highlighted in this book, the problem about the family unit of assessment. As Parker says:

> Economists have an annoying habit of assuming (without saying so) that money within the family flows equitably between its different members as though guided by an invisible hand, hence that living standards within families are homogenous. (Parker 1989: 145)

She goes on to quote an OECD report on negative income tax (NIT):

> There is a general agreement that the family should be the basic unit of any NIT plan, as the extent of any individual's economic welfare depends on the joint income of the economic unit to which he belongs. If the individual members of a family are allowed to file separate tax returns, some members may qualify for a net benefit whereas, when taken as a unit, the family's joint income would be deemed adequate. The family is probably the closest approximation to an ideal welfare unit. (OECD 1974: 29)

There is no intrinsic reason, however, why a negative income tax scheme could not be constructed on an individual basis, including both spouses and children as tax–benefit units. This idea does, however, sit a little oddly with a policy innovation principally advocated by the New Right, who want to see state involvement in welfare reduced rather than increased. An individually-based negative income tax system requires a very large number of separate means tests. Nevertheless it is worth bearing in mind that, at the same time as family means testing is becoming more and more salient in Mrs Thatcher's Britain, the tax system is moving in April 1990 to an individual assessment basis.

On top of all the other potential complications there is, as with the existing system, the question of what is to be done about the incidence of variable housing costs. Again, of course, negative income tax can take this into account by including housing costs within the definition of the individual's minimum needs, but this too adds complications to the decision process. We have also seen that the history of housing benefit has been one in which benefit entitlements have risen in line with increasing housing costs, with severe consequences for public expenditure. So we see that, in our negative income tax model, where the presentation started with the simple idea of a guaranteed £50 per week, the picture would be very different if it is a guaranteed £50 per week with adjustments for a variety of other needs plus housing costs which determines the starting-point for the whole system.

To summarize, we find that the advocates of negative income tax offer us a simple system to replace the horrifying complexity of our present reality. However, when we pause a little to look at the details of the system that they are offering us we find that they may well have to build in many of the complexities which we already experience within our existing system. Failure to build in those complexities will have the consequence of creating a system which operates with a national minimum which is horrifyingly low for many individuals. On the other hand, success in achieving a basic rate which makes many of the complex adjustments unnecessary will imply a basic rate that is high and accordingly one that requires either a very steep taper or very substantial contributions from those individuals in the fortunate position to be merely taxpayers.

The *basic income* or *social dividend* alternative for the reform of social security is illustrated in Figure 9.3. This involves

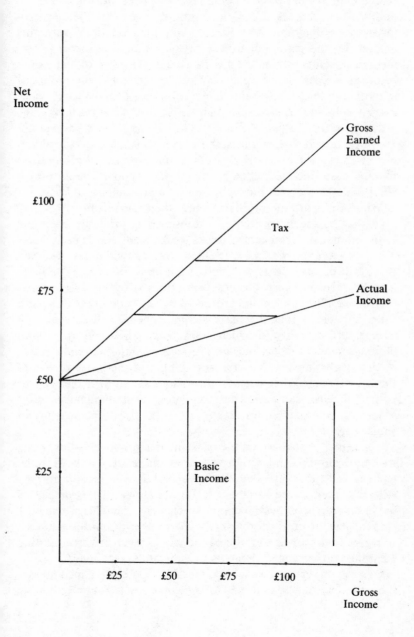

*Figure 9.3   Relationship between gross income and net income
with a basic income, or social dividend, scheme*

providing a basic minimum income for all, rather than trying to
provide a system of levelling up for those on low earned incomes.
In the diagram the basic income level has been drawn at the £50
point which was used for the minimum level in the negative
income tax diagram. All citizens would be provided with this
income by the state, regardless of their other resources. Basic
income schemes are normally based on the idea of individual
incomes and do therefore get away from the difficult problems
about family means tests and family insurance benefits which were
discussed in an earlier section. These types of schemes then leave
individuals free to earn incomes to supplement their basic state-
provided incomes. Obviously there is a substantial cost problem
here which must be met by a substantial tax rate. We therefore
find in basic income schemes that our diagonal line is drawn
sharply down towards the right by the imposition of taxation.

What, then, are the problems about the basic income proposal?
One that has secured greatest attention has probably been the
criticism that such a scheme attacks work incentives. If individuals
are guaranteed incomes sufficient to live on without work then
there will be no incentive to do certain kinds of work. The basic
income advocates turn this criticism into a virtue by arguing that
this will result in undesirable forms of work becoming better-paid.
They also argue that the basic income scheme will fit very well
with a future reality in which work is comparatively rare, with
large numbers of individuals unable to get regular work and much
of the available work only part-time. One of the great virtues of
the basic income scheme is that it provides a model for the support
of part-time workers and therefore provides a very much better
scheme than exists at present for, for example, the support of
single parents.

There is a sense in which the basic income proposal is Beveridge
without insurance and without the controls relating to work. One
can see the Beveridge benefits as forms of basic income for the
sick, the unemployed and the elderly, and above all of course child
benefit is a form of 'basic income' for children. The difference here
is that basic income is also available to adults without them having
to prove that they are in one of the categories for which existing
insurance or contingent benefits are currently available.

Despite its very different characteristics to negative income tax,
some of the objections to negative income tax also apply to basic

income. If the basic income is to be set at a sufficiently high level to cope with all the variations of individual need then it must be set at a fairly high level, and its consequences for taxation must be substantial. Once again housing costs could well be a problem for this type of scheme, although it should be noted that there have been advocates of basic housing allowances. This is a basic income-type benefit specifically for individual housing costs, enabling individuals to have some baseline support on top of which they may make additional commitments in seeking provision for their housing needs. However, some of the more practical advocates of basic income have acknowledged that it may be necessary to retain a means-tested housing benefit to cope with the housing cost problem, precisely because otherwise the scheme would require very high tax rates (Parker 1989).

To summarize, we therefore encounter, once again, the problem of judging an ideal menu without prices. A basic income scheme providing a very good level of minimum income will require very substantial taxation to pay for it. An inadequate basic income scheme on the other hand is likely to require a variety of subsidiary, probably means-tested, benefits to support it. Again the reality may be one in which we would undergo a substantial administrative turmoil as basic income was phased in and find at the end of it that we had a benefit system not greatly dissimilar to the system we have already.

Picking up that last theme, there is a sense, as has already been suggested, in which negative income tax represents the logical development of our already elaborate means-tested system, and basic income represents the logical development of the Beveridge ideal. In fact, we find that in Britain over the past few years there has been a significant group of critics of the social security system who have argued that the right road for reform lies in a restatement of the Beveridge principles in the context of the needs of our own age (Lister 1975; Deacon and Bradshaw 1983; National Consumer Council 1984; Hills 1988). This is probably best described as the 'new Beveridge' approach rather than the 'back to Beveridge' approach, since it offers a substantial advance on the original Beveridge design. Central to this approach has been the argument for the improvement of the insurance benefits, increasing their basic values and eliminating the fact that the unemployment insurance benefit exhausts. There has been quite substantial argument here about the extent to which the insurance contribution principle should itself be maintained. On the one side it is argued that it is a rather administratively ponderous and regressive tax, associated in many people's minds with the experience of paying for promised future benefits without any guarantee of support at the other end. It has also been associated with, and partly discredited by, some of the anomalies about insurance in the context of means testing which were discussed above. Those who feel like this, including myself, would argue that we should have instead contingent benefits and abolish the elaborate charade of insurance collection. This would involve acknowledging that National Insurance is really just another form of income tax. The alternative view is that insurance helps to keep the scheme politically acceptable. The idea that individuals are explicitly paying insurance for themselves against future shortfalls in income helps to secure attachment to the scheme as a whole. Politicians do seem to find it more acceptable to increase insurance contributions than to increase income tax rates.

Other features of the case for 'new Beveridge' are the abolition of the family assumptions in relation to benefit. They would have to be replaced, as suggested above, by a recognition of either benefit-sharing or various home and care responsibility additions if the insurance principle were to be maintained. On the other hand, the abandonment of the insurance principle would make it easier to deal with these issues. So far as childcare is concerned, it is particularly important to the advocates of the 'new Beveridge' approach to maintain and strengthen child benefit, and to add to child benefit itself a benefit to pay for childcare or to enable carers to be reimbursed for the cost of staying at home to look after their own children. It is only by an approach of this kind that it will be possible to reduce the role of means-tested benefits for the heads of single-parent families. The new Beveridge design also requires very much better provision for disabled people, with a need for them to have the resources to enable them to pay for carers. Again, there are alternatives here between a system of benefits for carers or a system of benefits for disabled people to enable them to pay for carers. The case for the latter is that it enables disabled people to make their own choices. Finally, it is very important for the 'new Beveridge' design to ensure that there is a universal coverage by the pension scheme. There is of course, already, virtually universal coverage by the original Beveridge scheme. What is less satisfactory is the complex structure of benefits over and above the basic pension scheme. The introduction of the State Earnings-Related Pension Scheme was accompanied by arrangements for individuals to contract out. Whilst developments in the 1980s have eliminated some of the problems deriving from contracting out – notably the problem that many pensions were not effectively portable from one occupation to another – the 1986 Act introduced a new set of problems in attracting many individuals to enter private schemes whose ultimate yields may be unsatisfactory. The latter Act also weakened the State Earnings-Related Pension Scheme itself. A comprehensive 'new Beveridge' social security system clearly needs to ensure that there are satisfactory pensions across the board, and in particular satisfactory pensions for women who have spent substantial parts of their lives in caring roles or in insecure employment. Although obviously in theory this issue can apply to men as well, it is stated here in terms of women's position, since in practice the numbers of men whose work histories trap them into inadequate pension situations are much fewer.

Finally, a note is appropriate on the relationships of all three approaches to benefits reform to the recent tendency of the government to 'privatize' social security by encouraging private pensions and requiring private employers to provide sickness and maternity support. The advocates of the 'new Beveridge' ideal would clearly like to reverse this development, if not by specifically abolishing private schemes then at least by strengthening related public schemes. Negative income tax, by contrast, is generally seen as a subsistence alternative for the social minority (class three in the earlier analysis) who lack the means to enter private social security schemes. Basic income schemes seem to fit, in general, between these two extremes. Just as they allow for earnings as additions to basic income so too do they leave room for earnings related private 'insurance'.

CONCLUSIONS

This final chapter has ended by bringing together for comparison with the problems of the present system three ideal models for the future. The 'new Beveridge' model has strong links with the social administration tradition. Negative income tax, with its quest for a more efficient approach to necessary (in many cases the minimum necessary) income redistribution has particular links with the economic tradition of policy advocacy. Basic income is a bit of a hybrid, a product of quite a long line of 'lateral' thinkers on social security dating at least as far back as one of Beveridge's critics, Lady Juliet Rhys Williams (1943). However, in the introductory chapter, and elsewhere in the book, readers have been urged to address, alongside the arguments of policy advocates, issues about the politics of social security and about the way the system is implemented. In summing up let us bring these considerations to bear on the alternative models.

Three particular points need to be made: about the nature of policy change in a society like Britain; about the importance of political support for innovation; and about the ways implementation processes may change and modify policies.

First, it is important to recognize that policy change is characteristically incremental. The biggest sequence of changes with which this book has been concerned occurred in a very abnormal period in political history, at the end of a devastating war and at a time when there seems to have been a tremendous will for change (Addison 1977), yet even these changes – the Beveridge reforms – built upon an already elaborate social insurance system. So the challenge to the advocates of our three new scenarios is to ask: can you envisage a series of incremental steps to your ideal and ensure protection of those steps from interference – from 'loser' groups, as a consequence of political changes to the government and so on – along the line? That challenge is the most severe for the most radical of the three schemes, basic income.

Negative income tax advocates can regard the 1986 Act as a step in their direction. Subsequent stages could involve the progressive weakening of National Insurance and child benefit so that means testing moved more and more towards the 'centre-stage' for the poor. The biggest hurdle, on which more will be said below, would be the reorientation of the tax system, and the need for development of more coherent policies for people close to the 'threshold' where benefit stops and tax starts. Without that, such evolution as does occur will simply transform the 'three-class' situation described earlier in the chapter into a two-class one, with the middle group squeezed out and the difficulties in moving from the 'lower' to the 'upper' class much intensified.

Conversely, 'new Beveridge' advocates require a series of steps which probably start, as groups like the Child Poverty Action Group recognize, with the enhancement of child benefit so that the basic costs of children are covered by the state for families in and out of work alike. Then the improvement of the insurance benefits can follow, by gradually increasing their coverage and probably letting their contributory roots 'decay'. The main problems about these steps lie in their costs, which create problems about the support for them and their vulnerability to political reversal, topics considered further below. Full employment is most important for this approach, just as it was recognized by Beveridge to be important for social insurance in the first place.

The introduction of basic income is much more difficult to envisage in incremental terms. Parker suggests that two 'big phases' of change are needed. These are difficult to summarize, but require some very careful interrelated changes to both benefits and taxes. If they are seen as too 'big' politically, the consequences must be some changes and not others. Surely the major danger with this scheme is simplification of benefits, offering a kind of basic income which is too low, whilst politicians baulk at the costly radical changes.

Moving now to the second question about the politics of change: the issue of political support. In some respects, the three models of change already have actual or potential political party allies. Negative income tax has caused a good deal of interest in Conservative circles; Labour is still to some extent wedded to the Beveridge model; and the various small parties seem interested in basic income. If this sounds a little like oblique advice to betting people to put their money on negative income tax, it must be acknowledged that negative income tax has the enormous advantage of continuing the shift in the means test direction and having the least public expenditure implications. Its main disadvantages lie *not* in problems of securing a powerful coalition of economic interests for its acceptance *but* in overcoming its implementation problems. These will be dealt with later.

Political support for the other two options must be expected to come from movements with egalitarian ideals. This is a view which seems to be contradicted to some degree by some of the supporters of basic income. Jordan has seen basic income as an option with appeal to both the Left and Right (Jordan 1985). However, surely any version on which there was a consensus would tend to turn out to be very limited in its taxation and redistribution implications? There are simple ways, as the Heath government discovered when it flirted with a version of basic income (HMSO 1972) in the early 1970s, of channelling a little more money to the working poor than taking up the whole tax and benefits systems by the roots!

Inasmuch as both basic income and 'new Beveridge' involve radical innovations of an egalitarian kind, both schemes have to face massive vested interests. Of the two the 'new Beveridge' option has the advantage of building on a cherished ideal from the past. The original Beveridge scheme had strong trade union support. Is this important for a 'new Beveridge' scheme? In the 'three-class' analysis of social security used earlier, the middle group were seen as the main beneficiaries of social insurance. The 'new Beveridge' model involves enlarging that group by admissions from the third group, for which the first group must be expected to pay. The Beveridge scheme was, in many respects, the highpoint of the political achievements of the organized British working class. The critical political questions to be answered, which are beyond the scope of this book, are first, to what extent the organized working class (in a comparatively traditional sense) is still a potential political force, and, second, if it is, will it form an effective coalition with other interests important for social security reform, particularly women's interest groups? To repeat a point made above, full employment is surely important if such a coalition is to be realized. The alternative scenario here is one in which those in secure employment come increasingly to see their security as depending upon semi-private employment-related schemes, and have little interest in joining with less secure groups in society to support state schemes.

In the light of these remarks the prospects for basic income must seem even more uncertain. In many ways, as an ideal, it is a scenario for a less-than-fully-employed society. It looks, therefore, for redistribution from those with opportunities to work to those with very limited, temporary and perhaps part-time, work opportunities. It requires a politically unlikely coalition of the insecure and the secure.

Finally, the third question about implementation which is in many respects subsidiary to the large political issues raised by the other two questions, must be answered briefly. The main observations on this are directed towards the negative income tax option. Its potential implementation problems have already been outlined. We know that tax and benefit integration is already regarded as difficult because of the extreme separation of the two systems of administration. However, the radical Right shows an increased reluctance to be put off by civil servants who argue that changes are administratively too difficult. Nevertheless, negative income tax surely imposes an amazingly heavy burden on administration and citizens alike. Coming, as the idea largely does, from advocates of cutting public expenditure it surely cannot be expected to operate with a high basic level and a gentle taper rate. Yet, without these, many of the issues about fine-tuning and about interactions with other public policies, discussed in the previous two chapters, will surely loom large. As pointed out earlier, it is odd that, while negative income tax is generally envisaged as involving a family means test, income tax is being moved onto an individual basis. Would politicians of the radical Right readily countenance an elaborate universal means test which, much of its time, would be shifting resources around within families?

In other words both 'new Beveridge' and basic income have advantages in that the challenges they pose for implementation are comparatively simple. The more money allocation decisions can be based upon simple criteria, and the more social security systems are able to provide individuals with adequately sized incomes and leave them to worry about the 'fine-tuning' problems of income expenditure, the fewer the implementation problems. But, to be fair, it has already been pointed out that this would not occur if basic incomes were set too low. Similarly 'new Beveridge' schemes are only worthwhile if the insurance or contingent benefits they provide are of adequate size; that is the current problem with the 'old' Beveridge scheme.

That is surely the most important note on which to draw this book to a close. Intellectuals may endlessly debate ideal schemes for social security, but the most important issues for the poor are about the adequacy of benefits. Most of the worst problems of any benefit scheme disappear if the benefit rates are generous. It is the quest for social, economic and administrative efficiency in social security against a background of a tightly controlled budget that is the source of so many of the problems analysed in this book.

To be adequate, each of the three alternative models would have to be expensive. Negative income tax is the option that tends to be advocated by those who want to keep public expenditure to a minimum, but in practice if really satisfactory transfers of income to the poor were to be achieved, and a severe poverty trap problem were to be avoided, then there would be, even for that scheme, a substantial cost problem. In relating all our models to political reality therefore, we must recognize that social security systems carry substantial public expenditure costs. The experience of the last 10 years of attack upon the social security system has clearly been motivated by the extent to which social security expenditure growth has figured so strikingly in the growth of public expenditure in general. As an advocate of improved social security, I cannot but reflect pessimistically that there are enormous political obstacles in the path of that improvement. Whatever the devices to convince the public that they are getting value for money, whether they be, as in the past, the insurance principle or, as advocated by the new Right, the guarantee of efficiency embodied in negative income tax, the fact is that ways have to be found to convince the electorate that state social security is something for which we all need to pay substantial taxes. In current debates about social security a great deal is made about changing dependency ratios. Above all, it is pointed out that, in the first quarter of the next century, the ratio of the working-age population to the non-working-age population will shift in a way which is markedly unfavourable to those of working age as the 'providers'. These predictions depend, of course, upon assumptions about normal retirement ages, which could well be refuted. However, if we accept them as they stand we have to recognize that the future that is being outlined, in demographic terms, is one in which there will be the need for substantial transfer of resources from the working population to the dependent population. This has been seen as a problem for state social security. What it is important to remember is that it is a problem whether or not we have a good state system. If, for example, we had no state pension system whatsoever but did have a large number of private schemes we would still have the situation in which the dependent elderly were drawing resources extensively out of private schemes and therefore imposing a substantial drain upon the resources produced by the working population. It is one of the myths about our society, unfortunately propagated by our leading politicians, that the economy of a country is exactly like the economy of an individual household. The reality is different. In households we may save to protect our future. In the economy as a whole, when those who have saved draw upon their savings in the future they will draw upon the resources being created by the working population of that time. When we save we do not save cans of beans, we save money (or even more precisely promises of money!) to enable us to buy the cans of beans being produced by future workers.

In other words, while there are very real problems about the preservation of a satisfactory state system of social security, it should *not* be accepted that, in the absence of a substantial state social security system, the problems of dependency – expressed both in terms of individual suffering and in terms of the complications for the economy – will go away. State-provided social security offers a rational approach to the solution of dependency problems. Whilst it is doubtful whether our present muddle is, in these terms, rational, it offers us, whichever way we may want to take it in terms of the future models discussed above, some of the rudiments of an approach to rational solutions to these problems.

References

Abel-Smith, B. and Townsend, P. (1965), *The Poor and the Poorest*, London: Bell.

Achenbaum, W.A. (1986), *Social Security: Visions and Revisions*, Cambridge: Cambridge University Press.

Addison, P. (1977), *The Road to 1945*, London: Quartet Books.

Adler, M. and Asquith, S. (eds.) (1981), *Discretion and Welfare*, London: Heinemann.

Atkinson, A.B. (1969), *Poverty in Britain and the Reform of Social Security*, Cambridge: Cambridge University Press.

Audit Commission (1986), *Making a Reality of Community Care*, London: HMSO.

Bacon, R. and Eltis, W. (1976), *Britain's Economic Problem: Too Few Producers*, London: Macmillan.

Banting, K.G. (1979), *Poverty, Politics and Policy*, London: Macmillan.

Berthoud, R. (1985), *The Examination of Social Security*, London: Policy Studies Institute.

Beveridge, Sir W. (1942), *Social Insurance and Allied Services*, Cmd. 6406, London: HMSO.

Booth, C. (1903), *Life and Labour of the People of London*, (17 vols), London: Macmillan.

Bowley, A.L. and Burnett-Hurst, A.R. (1915), *Livelihood and Poverty*, London: King.

Bowley, A.L. and Hogg, M.H. (1925), *Has Poverty Diminished?*, London: King.

Branson, N. (1979), *Poplarism*, London: Lawrence and Wishart.

Brittan, S. (1977), *The Economic Consequences of Democracy*, London: Temple Smith.

Buchanan, J. and Tullock, G. (1962), *The Calculus of Consent*, Ann Arbor: University of Michigan Press.

Bull, D. (1980), 'The anti-discretion movement in Britain: fact or phantom' in *Journal of Social Welfare Law*.

Cooper, S. (nd) 'Observations in supplementary benefit offices', unpublished.

Deacon, A. (1976), *In Search of the Scrounger*, London: Bell.

Deacon, A. (1978), 'The scrounging controversy', *Social and Economic Administration*, **12(2)**.

Deacon, A. and Bradshaw, J. (1983), *Reserved for the Poor*, Oxford: Martin Robertson.

Department of Employment (1971), *People and Jobs*, London: Deparment of Employment.

Department of Employment (1988), *Training for Employment*, London: HMSO.

Department of Health and Social Security (1978), *Social Assistance*, London: DHSS.

Department of Social Security (1987), *Social Security Statistics*, London: HMSO.

Dilnot, A.W., Kay, J.A. and Morris, C.N. (1984), *The Reform of Social Security*, Oxford: Clarendon Press.

Donnison, D. (1979), 'Social policy since Titmuss', *Journal of Social Policy*, **8(2)**.

Donnison, D. (1982), *The Politics of Poverty*, Oxford: Martin Robertson.

Ellis, B. (1989), *Pensions in Britain*, London: HMSO.

Field, F. (1972), *One Nation: The Conservatives' record since June 1970*, Poverty pamphlet 12, London: CPAG.

Fimister, G. (1986), *Welfare Rights Work in Social Services*, Basingstoke: Macmillan Educational.

Firth Report (1987), *Public Support for Residential Care*, Report of a Joint Central and Local Government Working Party, London: DHSS.

Friedman, M. (1962), *Capitalism and Freedom*, Chicago: University of Chicago Press.

Friedman, M. and Friedman, R. (1981), *Free to Choose*, Harmondsworth: Penguin Books.

Gilbert, B.B. (1966), *The Evolution of National Insurance in Great Britain*, London: Michael Joseph.

Gilbert, B.B. (1970), *British Social Policy 1914–1939*, London: Batsford.

Glendinning, C. and Millar, J. (eds.) (1987), *Women and Poverty in Britain*, Brighton: Wheatsheaf.

Golding, P. and Middleton, S. (1982), *Images of Welfare*, Oxford: Martin Robertson.

Gordon, P. and Newnham, A. (1985), *Passport to Benefits?*, London: CPAG.

Gough, I. (1979), *The Political Economy of the Welfare State*, London: Macmillan.

Hall, P., Land, H., Parker, R. and Webb, A. (1975), *Change, Choice and Conflict in Social Policy*, London: Heinemann.

Ham, C. and Hill, M. (1984), *The Policy Process in the Modern Capitalist State*, Brighton: Wheatsheaf.

Handler, J. (1973), *The Coercive Social Worker*, Chicago: Rand McNally.

Hansard, 17.11.1955, para. 795.

Harris, J. (1972), *Unemployment and Politics 1886–1914*, London: Oxford University Press.

Harris, J. (1977), *William Beveridge: a biography*, Oxford: Clarendon Press.

Harris, R. and Seldon, A. (1979), *Overruled on Welfare*, London: Institute of Economic Affairs.

Hennock, E.P. (1987), *British Social Reform and German Precedents*, Oxford: Clarendon Press.

Hill, M. (1969), 'The exercise of discretion in the National Assistance Board', *Public Administration*, **47**, pp.75–90.

Hill, M. (1984), 'The Implementation of Housing Benefit', *Journal of Social Policy*, **13(3)**, pp. 297–320.

Hill, M. and Bramley, G. (1986), *Analysing Social Policy*, Oxford: Blackwell.

Hill, M. and Laing, P. (1979), *Social Work and Money*, London: Allen and Unwin.

Hills, J. (1988), *Changing Tax*, London: CPAG.

HMSO (1961), *Housing in England and Wales*, London: HMSO.

HMSO (1966), *Prices and Incomes Standstill: period of severe restraint*, Cmnd. 3604, London: HMSO.

HMSO (1972), *Proposals for a Tax-Credit System*, Cmnd. 5116, London: HMSO.

HMSO (1985), *Reform of Social Security*, Cmnd. 9517, London: HMSO.

HMSO (1987), *Housing: The Government's Proposals*, Cm. 214, London: HMSO.

HMSO (1988), *Community Care: agenda for action*, (Griffiths Report), London: HMSO.

HMSO (1989), *Social Trends 19*, London: HMSO.

HMSO (1989), *The Government's Expenditure Plans 1989–90 to 1991–92: Social Security*, Cm. 615, London: HMSO.

Housing Benefit (General) Regulations (1987), reg. 11.

Howe, L.E.A. (1985), 'The "deserving" and the "undeserving": practice in an urban, local social security office', *Journal of Social Policy*, **14**.

Hvinden, B. (1989), 'Interorganisational relations in pursuit of social security', paper given to International Seminar on the Sociology of Social Security, Edinburgh.

Jones, B. (1989), 'Section one: at the crossroads', *Benefits Research*, **3**, pp. 22–25.

Jordan, B. (1974), *Poor Parents*, London: Routledge.

Jordan, B. (1985), *The State*, Oxford: Blackwell.

Jordan, B. (1987), *Rethinking Welfare*, Oxford: Blackwell.

Joseph, K. and Sumption, J. (1979), *Equality*, London: John Murray.

Kemp, P. (1988), *The Future of Private Renting*, Salford: University of Salford.

Kopsch, H. (1970), *The Approach of the Conservative Party to Social Policy During World War Two*, University of London, Ph.D. thesis.

Leach, S.N. (1981), 'Relationships between supplementary benefits and social services departments', *Policy and Politics*, **9(3)**, pp. 349–71.

Le Grand, J. (1982), *The Strategy of Equality*, London: Allen and Unwin.

Lipsky, M. (1980), *Street-level Bureaucracy*, New York: Russell Sage.

Lister, R. (1975), *Social Security: the case for reform*, Poverty pamphlet 22, London: CPAG.

Lister, R. (1979), *The No-cost No-benefit Review*, Poverty pamphlet 39, London: CPAG.

Lister, R. (1987), *There is an Alternative: reforming social security*, London: CPAG

Lister, R. and Emmett, T. (1976), *Under the Safey Net*, Poverty pamphlet 25, London: CPAG.

Loveland, I. (1987), 'Politics, organisation and the environment: influences on the exercise of administrative discretion within the housing benefits scheme', *Journal of Social Welfare Law*.

Loveland, I. (1988), 'Housing benefit: administrative law and administrative practice', *Public Administration*, **66(1)**, pp. 57–75.

MacGregor, S. (1981), *The Politics of Poverty*, London: Longman.

McCarthy, M. (1986), *Campaigning for the Poor*, London: Croom Helm.

McClements, L.D. (1978), *The Economics of Social Security*, London: Heinemann.

McLennan, G. (1989), *Marxism, Pluralism and Beyond*, Cambridge: Polity Press.

McKenzie, N. (ed.) (1958), *Conviction*, London: Macgibbon and Kee.

Mack, J. and Lansley, S. (1985), *Poor Britain*, London: Allen and Unwin.

Marsden, D. (1973), *Mothers Alone*, Harmondsworth: Penguin Books.

Meade, J.E. (1978), *The Structure and Reform of Direct Taxation*, London: Institute of Fiscal Studies.

Millar, J., Cooke, K. and McLaughlin, E. (1989), 'The employment lottery: risk and social security benefits', *Policy and Politics*, **17(1)**, pp. 75–82.

Millar, J. and Glendinning, C. (1989), 'Gender and poverty', *Journal of Social Policy*, **18(3)**, pp. 363–82.

Minford, P. (1984), *State Expenditure: a study in waste*, Supplement to *Economic Affairs*, **4(3)**.

Ministry of Housing and Local Government (1963), *Housing*, Cmnd. 2050, London: HMSO, pp. 16.

Murray, C. (1984), *Losing Ground*, New York: Basic Books.

National Consumer Council (1984), *Of Benefit to All*, London: NCC.

Novak, T. (1984), *Poverty and Social Security*, London: Pluto.

Novak, T. (1988), *Poverty and the State*, Milton Keynes: Open University Press.

O'Connor, J. (1973), *The Fiscal Crisis of the State*, New York: St Martins Press.

OECD (1974), *Negative Income Tax*, Paris: OECD.

Ogus, A.I. and Barendt, E.M. (1988), *The Law of Social Security* (3rd edn.), London: Butterworths.

Packman, J. (1975), *The Child's Generation*, Oxford: Blackwell.

Parker, H. (1980), *Goodbye Beveridge*, London: Outer Circle Policy Unit.

Parker, H. (1989), *Instead of the Dole*, London: Routledge.

Prest, A. and Barr, N. (1986), *Public Finance*, London: Weidenfeld and Nicolson.

Rhys Williams, J. (1943), *Something to Look Forward to*, London: Macdonald.

Rose, H. (1981), 'Rereading Titmuss: the sexual division of welfare', *Journal of Social Policy*, **10(4)**, pp. 477–502.

Rose, M.E. (1972), *The Relief of Poverty 1934–1914*, London: Macmillan.

Rowntree, B.S. (1901), *Poverty: a study of town life*, London: Macmillan.

Rowntree, B.S. (1941), *Poverty and Progress*, London: Longmans.

Rowntree, B.S. and Lavers, G.R. (1951), *Poverty and the Welfare State*, London: Longmans.

Sinfield, A. (1978), 'Analyses in the social division of welfare', *Journal of Social Policy*, **7(2)**, pp. 129–56.

Sinfield, A. (1981), *What Unemployment Means*, Oxford: Blackwell.

Social Security Advisory Committee (1988), *Benefits for Disabled People: a strategy for change*, London: HMSO.

Stevenson, O. (1973), *Claimant or Client?*, London: Allen and Unwin.

Stewart, G. and Stewart, J. (1986), *Boundary Changes: social work and social security*, Poverty pamphlet 70, London: Child Poverty Action Group.

Thane, P. (1982), *The Foundations of the Welfare State*, London: Longman.

Titmuss, R.M. (1958), *Essays on the Welfare State*, London: Allen and Unwin.

Titmuss, R.M. (1960), *The Irresponsible Society*, Fabian Tract 323, London: Fabian Society.

Titmuss, R.M. (1968), *Commitment to Welfare*, London: Allen and Unwin.

Titmuss, R.M. (1971), 'Welfare rights, law and discretion', *The Political Quarterly*, **42**.

Townsend, P. (1975), *Sociology and Social Policy*, London: Allen Lane.

Townsend, P. (1979), *Poverty in the United Kingdom*, Harmondsworth: Penguin Books.

Townsend, P. and Davidson, N. (1982), *Inequalities in Health*, London: Penguin Books.

Valencia, M. and Jackson, M. (1979), 'Variation in provision of financial aid through social work', *Policy and Politics*, **7(1)**.

Veit-Wilson, J. (1986), 'Paradigms of poverty: a rehabilitation of B.S. Rowntree', *Journal of Social Policy*, **15(1)**, pp. 69–100.

Walker, C. (1983), *Changing Social Policy*, London: Bedford Square Press.

Walter, J.A. (1988), *Basic Income: escape from the poverty trap*, London: Marion Boyars.

Whitehead, M. (1988), 'The health divide', in *Inequalities in Health* (new edn.), London: Penguin Books.

Wilson, A.J. and Hill, M. (1988), 'Social workers and welfare rights', in *Social Services Research*, **(5)**.

Index